Site-Specific Art

Performance, Place and Documentation

Nick Kaye

Routledge
Taylor & Francis Group

LONDON AND NEW YORK

First published 2000
by Routledge
2 Park Square, Milton Park, Oxon, OX14 4RN

Simultaneously published in the USA and Canada
by Routledge
270 Madison Ave, New York, NY 10016

Reprinted 2001, 2003, 2004 (twice), 2006, 2007 (twice), 2008

Routledge is an imprint of the Taylor & Francis Group, an informa business

Typeset in Janson and Scala Sans
by Florence Production Ltd., Stoodleigh, Devon
Printed and bound in Great Britain
by Bell and Bain Ltd., Glasgow

British Library Cataloguing in Publication Data
A catalogue record for this book is available from the
British Library

Library of Congress Cataloging in Publication Data
A catalogue record for this book has been requested

ISBN 10: 0-415-18558-0 (hbk)
ISBN 10: 0-415-18559-9 (pbk)
ISBN 13: 978-0-415-18558-5 (hbk)
ISBN 13: 978-0-415-18559-2 (pbk)

For Gabriella

Contents

Notes on Contributors

Tim Etchells: the Artistic Director of Forced Entertainment, an ensemble of artists based in Sheffield, UK, who have been working together since 1984. The group's work ranges from touring theatre performances to gallery installations, pieces made for unusual sites, digital and broadcast media. Their work grows from project to project, using text, technology, soundtrack and other elements in varying degrees.

Forced Entertainment are committed to an ensemble practice, to building and maintaining a group which shares a history, performance skills and an equal involvement in the process of making new work. Company members are Tim Etchells (Artistic Director and Writer), Robin Arthur, Richard Lowdon (Designer), Claire Marshall, Cathy Naden, Terry O'Connor. Regular collaborators include Nigel Edwards (Lighting), John Avery (Music and Sound), Hugo Glendinning (Photographic and Installation Work). Associates to the company are Tim Hall and Sue Marshall (performers), Mary Agnes and Krell/Bytehaus (Digital Projects). Alongside this ensemble the group also involve artists from other disciplines, introducing fresh skills and invigorating the notion of what contemporary performance might be. Forced Entertainment's long-term commitment is not to specific formal strategies but simply to challenging and provocative art.

Forced Entertainment's work has toured widely in- the UK and in mainland Europe as well as visiting the USA, Canada and Lebanon. The group attracts regular funding from the Arts Council of England Drama Department, Sheffield City Council and Yorkshire Arts. Tim Etchells' book, *Certain Fragments: Forced Entertainment and Contemporary Performance*, was published by Routledge in 1999.

Julian Maynard Smith: a performance artist and co-founder of the London-based performance company Station House Opera. Previously making solo work, as well as performing with the influential British performance art company, The Ting: Theatre of Mistakes, he formed Station House Opera with Miranda Payne and Alison Urquhart in 1980 in order to develop a performance practice combining sculptural, architectural and theatrical elements. Following their first work, *Natural Disasters*, presented in London in 1980 and in Amsterdam in 1982, the company's performances have been seen widely in Europe, Japan, Australia and North America. Since their inception, Station House Opera have created more than twenty works for galleries, theatres and numerous outdoor sites. These include *Drunken Madness* (1983), in which performers were flighted within a system of interdependent platforms and pulleys, *Cuckoo* (1987) and *Bastille Dances* (1989), in which a company of forty performers created and dismantled an edifice of 8,000 breeze blocks over nine days. The company's more recent work has included the site-specific works *Limelight* (1995) and *The Salisbury Proverbs* (1997) as well as *Roadmetal, Sweetbread* (1999) which combines video and live performance.

Clifford McLucas: the Artistic Director of the Welsh performance company Brith Gof. Trained originally as an architect, McLucas joined Brith Gof in the late 1980s specifically to create large-scale, site-specific performance events. At this time, his contribution to the company manifested itself in a suite of three large-scale pieces. The first, *Goddodin*, a collaboration with Test Dept., the London-based industrial music collective, was premiered in Cardiff, Wales, in the old Rover car factory in the docklands area of the city. The performance was subsequently restaged in a working sand quarry in Polverigi, Italy, an old crane factory in Hamburg, Germany, and an ice hockey stadium in Frisland, the Netherlands. The second work, *Pax* of 1991–2, was performed in Cardiff, the Harland and Wolff shipbuilding yard in Glasgow, and the British Rail Station in Aberystwyth. *Haearn* (*Iron*), the third piece of the series, was created in 1993 for the Old British Coal Works in the small post-industrial town of Tredegar in South Wales. *Haearn* was created as a joint production between Brith Gof, the BBC and S4C. Subsequently, McLucas created *Y Pen Bas/Y Pen Dwfn* (*The Shallow End/The Deep End*) in Welsh-language and English-language versions solely for the television medium.

In the mid-1990s, McLucas sought to re-engage the company with its Welsh-language constituency. The work that was the medium for this new engagement was *Tri Bywyd* (*Three Lives*) of 1995. At this time, McLucas relocated a significant component of Brith Gof's operation to the University of Wales in Lampeter in order to embark on a series of site-specific works in non-urban locations.

The models developed in Brith Gof's recent works aim to develop notions of site-specificity into new arenas. Using technologies of site, discontinuous techniques of performance, and incorporating closed-circuit video as well as complex radio microphone relay systems, McLucas has sought to develop a contemporary theatrical practice within contexts that are often assumed to be 'traditional'. In this context, McLucas is committed to a culturally specific creative practice that can engage with real locations, histories and identities while resonating within wider international arenas. This practice is one which seeks ways of expressing and animating located identities not as simplified and essentialist narratives, but as fractured and negotiated, sophisticated strategies for survival.

Meredith Monk: a composer, singer, filmmaker, choreographer and director based in New York. A pioneer in what is now called 'extended vocal technique' and 'interdisciplinary performance', she is the fourth generation singer in her family. Since graduating from Sarah Lawrence College in 1964, she has created more than 100 works. Monk's contributions to the cultural landscape were recognised with the award of the prestigious McArthur 'Genius' award in 1995. This achievement was followed by a retrospective exhibition, *Meredith Monk: Archaeology of an Artist*, at the New York Public Library for the Performing Arts at Lincoln Center in 1996, and more recently, a major installation, *Art Performs Life*, at the Walker Arts Center.

Monk has received numerous awards throughout her career, including two Guggenheim Fellowships, a Brandeis Creative Arts Award, three Obies (including an award for Sustained Achievement), two Villager Awards, a Bessie for Sustained Creative Achievement, the 1988 National Music Theater Award, sixteen ASCAP Awards for Musical Composition and the

1992 Dance Magazine Award. She holds honorary Doctor of Arts degrees from Bard College, the University of the Arts, and the Juilliard School. Her recordings *Dolmen Music* (ECM New Series) and *Our Lady of Late: The Vanguard Tapes* (Wergo) were honoured with the German Critics Prize for Best Records in 1981 and 1986. Her music has been heard in numerous films, including *La Nouvelle Vague* by Jean-Luc Godard and *The Big Lebowski* by Joel and Ethan Coen.

In 1968 Monk founded The House, a company dedicated to an inter-disciplinary approach to performance. She formed Meredith Monk and Vocal Ensemble in 1978 to perform her unique musical compositions. Monk has made more than a dozen recordings, most of which are on the ECM New Series label, including her full-length opera, *ATLAS: an opera in three parts*, which premiered at the Houston Grand Opera in 1991. In March 1997, ECM released the CD *Volcano Songs*. She is also an accomplished filmmaker who has made a series of award-winning films including *Ellis Island* (1981) and her first feature, *Book of Days* (1988), which was aired on Public Broadcast Television, released theatrically, and selected for the Whitney Museum's Biennial.

In 1996, Monk created *The Politics of Quiet*, a music/theatre oratorio, and *A Celebration Service*, a non-sectarian worship service that melds her haunting vocal music and movement with spiritual texts drawn from two millennia. Monk's most recent production, *Magic Frequencies* (1998), is a science fiction chamber opera. A monograph on Monk's work, *Meredith Monk*, edited by Deborah Jowitt, was released by the Johns Hopkins University Press in 1997.

Michelangelo Pistoletto: shown work extensively in major solo and group exhibitions across Europe and North America since 1960. One of the principal proponents and shaping influences of the internationally signif-icant *arte povera* movement, Pistoletto has been a major influence on new art and experimental performance practices. His early work was defined in explorations of 'real space' and time-based processes in gallery installations frequently employing mirrors and Plexiglas. Pistoletto has consistently elaborated his concerns through diverse forms of work, including installation, sculpture, performance art, theatre and publication. In the late 1960s, he engaged directly with performance through his collaborations with other artists as part of the collective *Lo Zoo* (The Zoo). Pistoletto went on to develop performances including *Silenzio Rosa* (*Pink Silence*) for the 1976 Venice Biennale, a production of Beckett's *Neither* at the Teatro dell'Opera, Rome in 1977, and *Creative Collaboration* staged in collaboration with the general public at various sites in Atlanta, USA in 1979. In 1981, Pistoletto brought his ongoing collaboration with the town of Corniglia, in Liguria, to bear on his theatre work through the production of *Anno Uno* (*Year One*), written and staged by Pistoletto, and performed in the Teatro Quirino in Rome by the citizens of Corniglia. Pistoletto continues to develop his work across a variety of media and shows regularly in galleries across Europe and the USA. In 1999 the Museum of Modern Art in Oxford, UK, hosted a major retrospective exhibition of Pistoletto's mirror pieces, *Shifting Perspective* ('*I am the Other*'): *Mirror Work 1962–1992*. In tandem with this, Pistoletto created *New Work* (1976–99), a mixed-media installation, for the Henry Moore Foundation Studio, Dean Clough, Halifax, UK.

Acknowledgements

This book has been developed with the support of many individuals whose enthusiasm, interest, and contributions have shaped this project. I would like to begin by thanking the artists who have created the documentations which form such a very significant part of this work. Tim Etchells, Julian Maynard Smith, and Clifford McLucas have contributed fully and unfailingly to the project from the proposal stage, since which some considerable time has passed. Meredith Monk and Michelangelo Pistoletto have also made essential and extremely generous contributions to this book. I am extremely grateful to each of the artists who have collaborated with *Site-Specific Art*, whose value for me is closely tied to these exchanges. In this regard, I would especially like to thank Maria Pistoletto for her interest in and generous support of this project. I would also like to thank Michou Szabo of The House Foundation for his assiduous help in connection with Meredith Monk's contribution to the book and Professor Mike Pearson for his early interest and encouragement in relation to the documentation of Brith Gof's work.

Of particular value to the preparation of the book was a series of interviews conducted in 1996 and 1997 with artists whose work is addressed here. I would especially like to thank Giovanni Anselmo, Giuseppe Penone and Gilberto Zorio for their time and generosity in participating in interviews in Turin in December 1996. I would also like to thank Robert Morris for an interview in New York in April 1997. Each of these conversations directly influenced the course of this book's development. I am also very grateful to Gilberto Zorio for his kind permission to reproduce the image of *Luci* (1968) installed at the Stedelijk van Abbemuseum, Eindhoven, 1987, on the cover of this book.

This project has also received significant institutional support without which it could not have been completed. I would particularly like to thank the Arts Council of England for a grant for the commissioning of documentations by Tim Etchells, Clifford McLucas and Julian

Maynard Smith, and especially Bronac Ferran of the Live Arts Unit for her support in this regard. The University of Warwick allowed a period of sabbatical leave to develop my research, as well as providing a Research Travel Award for research in Amsterdam, Turin, London and Cardiff in 1996 and 1997. A British Academy award also supported a period of research in New York in April 1997.

I would also like to acknowledge the invaluable support of the staff and resources of the following libraries. In Aberystwyth: The National Library of Wales and especially Douglas Jones for picture research. In Amsterdam: the Library of the Stedelijk Museum and the archive and private library of the De Appel Foundation. In New York: the New York Public Library for the Performing Arts at Lincoln Center, the Jerome Robbins Archive of the Recorded Moving Image at Lincoln Center, the New York Public Library, the library of the Museum of Modern Art, and the library of Columbia University. In Turin: the library of the Galleria D'Arte Moderna.

On behalf of the contributing companies and artists, I would like to make the following acknowledgements. Forced Entertainment's production of *Nights In This City* in 1995 was financially supported by the Arts Council of England, Yorkshire and Humberside Arts and Sheffield City Council. It was presented in partnership with Sheffield theatres. The project was directed by Tim Etchells and performed by Robin Arthur, Terry O'Connor, Cathy Naden, Claire Marshall and Richard Lowdon. The text was by Tim Etchells and the company. A version of the project was made in Rotterdam, the Netherlands, during 1997 as a production of Forced Entertainment and Rotterdamse Schouwburg, with the support of Rotterdam Festivals, the British Council, Mondriaanstichting and RET. Brith Gof's *Tri Bywyd* was produced in association with the Aberystwyth Arts Centre, Theatr Felinfach and Theatr Mwldan and with the financial support of the Arts Council of Wales. The project was created in collaboration with Dawns Dyfed, the Department of Archaeology at the University of Wales, Lampeter, and Forest Enterprise at the Forestry Commission. Station House Opera's *The Bastille Dances* was co-produced by Théâtre de Cherbourg, LIFT London,

Zomerfestijn/Mickery Amsterdam and Festivals de Barcelona Olimpiades Cultural with funding from the British Council, ONDA France and the Arts Council of England. *The Salisbury Proverbs* was a Salisbury Festival Commission funded by the Arts Council of England.

Acknowledgements for the documentations presented in this volume are as follows. For Forced Entertainment's *Nights In This City* all text and images are copyright of Tim Etchells. Photographs for Michelangelo Pistoletto's *LE STANZE* are by Paolo Mussat Sartor with English translation of the text by Malcolm Skey, except for page 88 which is translated by Gabriella Giannachi. I am pleased to acknowledge that *LE STANZE* was first published in Italian and English by TAU/MA in Bologna. Michelangelo Pistoletto retains copyright over *LE STANZE*. The aerial photographs incorporated into *Ten Feet and Three Quarters of an Inch of Theatre* on pages 130 and 131 are ©Crown Copyright/MOD and are reproduced with the permission of the Controller of HMSO. The Ordnance Survey maps incorporated into pages 130, 131 and 132 are reproduced with kind permission of The Ordnance Survey NC/99/309. The image plan of Lletherneuadd Farm on page 132 is reproduced from *The Wreath on the Crown* by John Cole, with kind permission of the publishers Gwasg Gomer of Llandysul, Ceredigion. For Station House Opera's *The Bastille Dances*, all images are by Julian Maynard Smith, as are the line illustrations and the text for *The Salisbury Proverbs*. Photographs for *The Salisbury Proverbs* are ©Bob van Dantzig and are reproduced here with permission. I am grateful for permission from Barbara Moore, Beatriz Schiller, and Ruth Waltz, to reproduce the photographic material included in Meredith Monk's documentation. All other photographic images in this documentation are courtesy of The House Foundation for The Arts. Specific photo-credits are acknowledged in the text. I am also grateful to Brad Ensminger, who was commissioned as designer for this work, and Siri Engberg for permission to reproduce her texts.

In relation to my own writing, I am happy to acknowledge that parts of my discussion of Daniel Buren's work appear in an earlier article, 'Intermedia and Location', published in 2000 in *Degrés: Revue de*

Synthèse à Orientation Sémiologique, section 'b' pp. 1–17. An earlier version of my discussion of Fiona Templeton's work appears in my article 'Site/Intermedia' published in 1996 in *Performance Research* 1, 1: 63–9. My discussion of Robert Smithson's *Spiral Jetty* also draws on my essay-review of Gary Shapiro's 1995 volume *Earthwards: Robert Smithson and Art After Babel* (Berkeley, Cal.: University of California Press), published in 1997 in *Performance Research* 2, 2: 113–15. I am grateful to Dennis Oppenheim for his kind permission to reproduce images of *One Hour Run* (1968) and *Arm & Wire* (1969) in the chapter 'Materials'.

I would also like to extend my warm thanks to Lieselotte Giannachi-Mangels for her generous help with contacts, material and support in Turin. I would also like to thank Mrs Stein of the Christian Stein Gallery of Turin for her invaluable help in contacting artists whose work is of special importance to this book. I would like to thank Talia Rodgers at Routledge for her patience and enthusiasm in dealing with this project. Finally, I would like to acknowledge my considerable debt to Gabriella Giannachi, whose generous support throughout the duration of this project has extended from the translation of text and of interviews with Giovanni Anselmo, Giuseppe Penone and Gilberto Zorio, to many questions, conversations, as well as an unfailing encouragement, without which this book would certainly not have reached completion.

Introduction:
Site-specifics

'site': *substantive.* [. . .] local position [. . .] The place or position occupied by some specified thing. Frequently implying original or fixed position.
'site': **1.** *transitive.* To locate, to place. **2.** *intransitive.* To be situated or placed.

(Onions 1973)

This book is concerned with practices which, in one way or another, articulate exchanges between the work of art and the places in which its meanings are defined. Indeed, a definition of site-specificity might begin quite simply by describing the basis of such an exchange. If one accepts the proposition that the meanings of utterances, actions and events are affected by their 'local position', by the *situation* of which they are a part, then a work of art, too, will be defined in relation to its place and position. Reflecting this notion, semiotic theory proposes, straightforwardly, that reading implies 'location'. To 'read' the sign is to *have located* the signifier, to have recognised its place within the semiotic system. One can go on from this to argue that the location, in reading, of an image, object, or event, its positioning in relation to political, aesthetic, geographical, institutional, or other discourses, all inform what 'it' can be said to *be*.

Site-specificity, then, can be understood in terms of this process, while a 'site-specific work' might articulate and define itself through properties, qualities or meanings produced in specific relationships between an 'object' or 'event' and a position it occupies. After the 'substantive' notion of site, such site-specific work might even assert a 'proper' relationship with its location, claiming an 'original and fixed position' associated with what it *is*. This formulation echoes the sculptor Richard

Serra's response to the public debate, and legal action, over the removal of his 'site-specific' sculpture *Tilted Arc* of 1981. Offering a key definition of 'site-specific' work, Serra concluded simply and unequivocally that 'To move the work is to destroy the work' (Serra 1994: 194). To move the site-specific work is to *re-place* it, to make it *something else*.

In its origins in the minimalist sculpture of the 1960s, however, and while linked to an exposure of the object's situation, site-specificity presents a challenge to notions of 'original' or 'fixed' location, problematising the relationship between work and site. In reproducing in object-form the aesthetic of the supposedly empty 'White Cube' gallery-spaces (O'Docherty 1986) they occupied, the early unitary forms of Robert Morris and minimalist objects of artists such as Frank Stella and Donald Judd seemed intent on throwing the viewer's attention toward these simple, three-dimensional objects back upon itself. In his influential account of contemporary art's critique of the museum, *On the Museum's Ruins* (Crimp 1993), the critic Douglas Crimp recounts this 'attack on the prestige of both artist and artwork' in favour of the spectator's 'self-conscious perception of the minimal object' (Crimp 1993: 16–17). Arguing that it was this very 'condition of reception' which 'came to be known as site specificity', he concludes that minimalism's radicalism 'lay not only in the displacement of the artist-subject by the spectator-subject but in securing that displacement through the wedding of the artwork to a particular environment' (Crimp 1993: 16–17). 'Site-specificity', as Crimp defines it here, is not resolved into the special characteristics of the minimalist object's specific position, but occurs in a displacement of the viewer's attention toward the room which both she and the object occupy. Rather than 'establish its place', the minimalist object emphasises a transitive definition of site, forcing a self-conscious perception in which the viewer confronts her own effort 'to locate, to place' the work and so her own acting out of the gallery's function as the place for viewing.

The significance of minimalism to ideas of site-specificity, however, does not only lie in this equation with a condition of reception. For the critic and celebrated proponent of Modernist art, Michael Fried, arguing that 'the experience of literalist [minimal] art is of an object *in a situation* – one that, virtually by definition, *includes the beholder*' (Fried 1968: 125), minimalism enters into a quintessentially theatrical practice antithetical to the values of an autonomous art. In forcing an incursion of the time and space of viewing into the experience of the work, Fried argues, minimalism enters into a realm which 'lies *between* the arts', where '*art degenerates as it approaches the condition of theatre*' (Fried 1968: 141). In emphasising the transitory and ephemeral act of viewing *in* the gallery, minimalism enters into the theatrical and performative. Here, minimalism's site-specificity can be said to begin in sculpture, yet reveal itself in performance, a move which calls into question its formal as well as spatial location.

Beginning with these debates defined around minimalism, then, this book proposes a site-specificity linked to the incursion of performance into visual art and architecture, in strategies which work against the assumptions and stabilities of site and location, and which offer a context of practices and concepts through which site-specific theatre can be read. Just as this tie between performance and place is articulated through inter-disciplinary practices, so this volume proposes that site-specificity should be associated with an underlying concept of 'site', rather than with any given or particular *kind* of place or formal approach to site. In considering strategies which variously occupy urban and rural locations, which utilise found and constructed environments, as well as those occurring in conventional galleries and theatres, site-specific practices are identified, here, with a *working over* of the production, definition and *performance* of 'place'.

This emphasis on performance might also be prompted by a reconsideration of the operation of language in relation to location and site. Indeed, where the location of the signifier may be read as *being performed* by the reader, then the functioning of language provides an initial model for the performance of place.

In *The Practice of Everyday Life* (de Certeau 1984), the philosopher Michel de Certeau reflects on the relationship between 'place' and 'space'. Adopting the semiotician Ferdinand de Saussure's distinction

between the *langue*, the complex of rules and conventions which constitute a language, and the *parole*, the practice of speech in which these
rules are given expression, de Certeau reads 'place' as an ordered and
ordering system realised in 'spatial practices'. Just as Saussure understands the *langue* to be always realised *in practices*, yet never wholly
manifest in any particular linguistic expression or exchange, de Certeau
proposes that

> *space is a practiced place.* Thus the street geometrically defined by
> urban planning is transformed into a space by walkers. In the
> same way, an act of reading is the space produced by the practice
> of a particular place: a written text, i.e.: a place constituted by a
> system of signs.
>
> (de Certeau 1984: 117)

Defined by its internal stability, 'place', like the *langue*, is an exclusive
and self-regulating system of rules, 'an instantaneous configuration of
positions' (de Certeau 1984: 117), which enunciation or practice at once
realises and depends upon. As the order through which a practice
obtains location, it is this 'place' which ensures that practices make
sense. De Certeau states that:

> A place [*lieu*] is the order (of whatever kind) in accordance with
> which elements are distributed in relationships of coexistence. It
> thus excludes the possibility of two things being in the same
> location [*place*]. The law of the 'proper' rules in the place: the
> elements taken into consideration are *beside* one another, each
> situated in its own 'proper' and distinct location, a location it
> defines.
>
> (de Certeau 1984: 117)

The order and stability of place, however, is not a property of the
practices in which it is realised. De Certeau notes straightforwardly
that spatial practices may give multiple expressions to the stability and

orderliness, to the 'univocity', of place. Space, he suggests, 'occurs as the effect produced by the operations that orient it, situate it, temporalize it, and make it function in a polyvalent unity of conflictual programmes' (de Certeau 1984: 117). In this sense, de Certeau does not read place as *an order*, but as *an ordering system*, while spatial practices do not reproduce fragments of a given order, but operate as *ordering activities*, whether that activity be walking, reading, listening or viewing. Thus, different and even incompatible spaces may realise the various possibilities of a single place. Returning to the metaphor of language, de Certeau outlines a more complex situation, suggesting that

> in relation to place, space is like the word when it is spoken, that is, when it is caught in the ambiguity of an actualization, transformed into a term dependent upon many different conventions, situated as the act of a present (or of a time), and modified by the transformations caused by successive contexts. In contradistinction to the place, it has thus none of the univocity or stability of a 'proper'.
>
> (de Certeau 1984: 117)

Space, as a *practiced place*, admits of unpredictability. Rather than mirror the orderliness of place, space might be subject not only to transformation, but ambiguity. If space is like the word when it is spoken, then a single 'place' will be realised in successive, multiple and even irreconcilable spaces. It follows that, paradoxically, 'space' cannot manifest the order and stability of its place. Thus, in comparing 'pedestrian processes to linguistic formations' de Certeau states categorically that '[t]o walk is to lack a place. It is the indefinite process of being absent and in search of a proper' (de Certeau 1984: 103).

Caught in the act of enunciation, perpetually in the practiced place, the walker can never resolve the multiple and conflicting spaces of the city into the place itself. The walker is thus always in the process of *acting out*, of performing the contingencies of a particular spatial practice, which, although subject to the place, can never wholly realise or be resolved into this underlying order. For de Certeau, the modern city epitomises this transitory condition, producing an awareness of our perpetual performance of place but inability to come to rest in the stability of the 'proper'. He observes that:

> The moving about that the city multiplies and concentrates makes the city itself an immense social experience of lacking a place [. . .] The identity furnished by this place is all the more symbolic (named) because, in spite of the inequality of its citizens' positions and profits, there is only a population of passers-by, a network of residences temporarily appropriated by pedestrian traffic, a shuffling among pretences of the proper, a universe of rented spaces haunted by a nowhere or by dreamed-of places.
>
> (de Certeau 1984: 103)

In the city, de Certeau's walker realises the site in its transitive sense, always in the act or effort of locating, and never in the settled order, the 'proper place', of the location itself. As de Certeau indicates, even the attempt to fix location through the 'symbolic (named)' participates in this *movement*. Here, where space, like the spoken word, is realised in a practice which can never rest in the order it implies, so the representation offered by 'the word' *moves one on* from 'site'. Just as these spatial practices function in the *absence* of place, in their inability to realise the order and stability of the proper, so the 'symbolic (named)' is tied to the experience of lacking a place precisely because representation, by definition, presents itself in the *absence* of its object. It follows that, ironically, the 'symbolic (named)' is antithetical to the *presence* of the authentic or real place it would reveal. In his discussion of 'The Photographic Activity of Postmodernism', Crimp argues that '[t]he desire of representation exists only insofar as it can never be fulfilled, insofar as the original always is deferred. It is only in the absence of the original that representation can take place' (Crimp 1993: 119).

To represent the place, is, in this sense, and analogously to its practice, to construct a *removal* from it. Like any of the spatial practices de Certeau describes, however, this very moving on, which is reflected in minimalism's deflection and reversal of the gaze, also implies its own place. In this respect, this sense of mobility, of spaces or places defined in fluid, shifting and transient acts and relationships, reveals further ties between approaches to site through visual art and theatre.

In *Nights In This City*, first presented in the northern English industrial city of Sheffield in 1995 and subsequently relocated in Rotterdam, Holland, in 1997, the British company Forced Entertainment foreground their work's roots in the city. Admitted to a tour bus by a performer-hostess, an audience of fifty begin a 'strange tour of various locations in Sheffield' (Etchells 1995). As a soundtrack plays over its speakers, the bus climbs to Sky Edge, above the Manor Park estate, beyond which the city centre and its industrial and suburban sprawl reach out into the distance. Here, once the driver Ray has pointed out the place where he first worked in the city, his home, and 'the place where he was married fifteen years ago', the party is joined by Alan, a 'professional' tour guide seemingly worse-the-wear for drink, played by company member Richard Lowdon. As the bus criss-crosses various parts of the city, Alan offers a guide to its streets and landmarks which becomes progressively more distracted:

> We're going to be taking you south on Love Street, past the
> place where they're thinking of building a new McDonald's, and
> past the entrance to Knife Walk, so called on account of all the
> murders that are commonly done there [. . .] All the streets round
> here got named after famous football hooligans from history and
> all the buildings got named after ghosts and cleaning products
> and convicted kerb crawlers [. . .] Ladies and gentlemen welcome
> to Rome . . .

In their self-conscious manipulation of appropriated textual fragments, Forced Entertainment emphasise the constructed nature of role, identity and place. Reflecting their concerns with media and mediation, the group work, in their theatre performances, to heighten the artificiality of the elements they play through, allowing one 'fictional' moment to shift on to or be juxtaposed with another. Tim Etchells, who writes and directs for the company, suggests that such strategies foreground 'the inability of the performers to fully inhabit the texts and gestures which they perform' in an articulation of a sense that '[t]here's no utterance by anybody that isn't somehow a quotation of something else' (Kaye 1996: 244). Translated into an address to a real city, which, Etchells suggests, 'is both a map of space and a map of states of mind' (Etchells 1999: 77), the company engage in a 'writing over the city' which reflects the notion that 'The space that we really live in is a kind of electronically mediated one. And it feels like one's landscape – the source of one's images, the things that haunt you – are likely to be second, third, fourth-hand' (Kaye 1996: 236).

In this dream-like journey through Sheffield's backstreets and housing estates, the company play out the need to construct, build or state connections with a site or place. Yet through these incongruous representations of the city's spectacles, this journey evokes an inability to *rest* in the places toward which the audience's attention is directed. As a site-specific work, *Nights In This City* articulates a curious displacement from a site whose particularities cannot be easily or appropriately named. It is a displacement reflected in the approach to the re-siting of *Nights In This City* in Rotterdam in 1997, when company members elicited suggestions for a route by posing questions which implied generic narratives or events linked to dramatic themes: 'If you had killed someone and had to dump the body where would you take it?' 'If you had to say goodbye to a lover, where in this city would you most like to do it?' Like the performance itself, this process *acts out* a 'writing over' the site, a *moving on* from the real city inscribed into the very attempt to know it. In these ways, *Nights In This City* effects a twin movement over its site, at once moving its audience through the city, while playing out the effect of the 'symbolic (named)', in which this 'tour' perpetually *moves one on* from its object.

Yet this experience of lacking a place, or of a place characterised by mobility or movement, can be further articulated in relation to place and space. Extending the implication of de Certeau's reference to the 'symbolic (named)' in an analysis of the spaces of supermodernity, the anthropologist Marc Augé reflects on the notion of 'non-place'. Defining non-place in opposition to what he describes as anthropological place, Augé's analysis reflects distinctions between the transitive and substantive definitions of site. Thus, he notes that '[w]hen Michel de Certeau mentions "non-place", it is to allude to a sort of negative quality of place, an absence of the place from itself, caused by the name it has been given' (Augé 1995: 85).

While 'anthropological place', Augé states, 'is formed by individual identities, through complicities of language, local references, the unformulated rules of living know-how' (Augé 1995: 101), where one's location or position is *known*, 'non-place' is produced in a *passing over* of place. More specifically, Augé argues, '"non-place" designates two complementary but distinct realities: spaces formed in relation to certain ends (transport, transit, commerce, leisure), and the relations that individuals have with these spaces' (Augé 1995: 78). Here, non-place is characterised by a projection forward, in the individual's relationship with this moving on, and so in a mobility which suppresses the differences in which anthropological places are established. Non-place, Augé suggests, is realised in travelling by or through anthropological places and so in a process of displacement. In this way, Augé proposes that:

> Space, as frequentation of *places* rather than a place stems in effect from a double movement: the traveller's movement, of course, but also a parallel movement of the landscapes which he catches only in partial glimpses, a series of 'snapshots' piled hurriedly into his memory and, literally, recomposed in the account he gives of them [. . .] Travel [. . .] constructs a fictional relationship between gaze and landscape.
>
> (Augé 1995: 86)

Here, too, in this frequentation of places which specifically defines the journey, Augé argues, the spectator's gaze is subject to a deflection or reversal, where, in this passing over, by or through *places* 'the individual feels himself to be a spectator without paying much attention to the spectacle. As if the position of spectator were the essence of the spectacle, as if basically the spectator in the position of a spectator were his own spectacle' (Augé 1995: 86).

Nights In This City, then, can be read as articulating this movement and reversal. Alan's narrative, the promise of coincidences between the fictions of the text and the happenstance of the street, as well as the thought that amid this flow of the everyday there may be incidents constructed for the audience, demands that one looks for the piece *outside*. Yet in looking out, through the trace of one's own reflection in the window, this gaze is returned by passers-by and, on one occasion, performers, who simply *look back* as the coach winds its way through areas where such a journey is explicitly out of place. Here, the tour-bus, like the gallery-space into which the minimalist object intervenes, is realised and reflected back to the viewer as a *place for looking*, provoking a self-conscious perception over which these representations of the city are played. For Augé, this self-regarding gaze suggests precisely a writing over of place through the anticipated image, a *moving on* epitomised by contemporary travel. Augé notes that:

> A lot of tourism leaflets suggest this deflection, this reversal of
> the gaze, by offering the would-be traveller advance images of
> curious or contemplative faces, solitary or in groups, gazing
> across infinite oceans, scanning ranges of snow-capped mountains
> or wondrous urban skylines: his own image in a word, his
> anticipated image, which speaks only about him but carries
> another name (Tahiti, Alpe d'Huez, New York). The traveller's
> space may thus be the archetype of *non-place*.
>
> (Augé 1995: 86)

Yet non-place, as Augé describes it, and as it may be reflected in the displacements of minimalism or the viewer's movement through this city, is not in any simple way the antithesis or negation of place. Indeed, non-place is defined, first of all, in relation to place, even as that relationship is one of displacement. Thus Augé points to the implication of non-place *in* place and vice versa, stating that:

> Place and non-place are rather like opposed polarities: the first is never completely erased, the second never totally completed; they are like palimpsests on which the scrambled game of identity and relations is ceaselessly rewritten. But non-places are the real measure of our time.
>
> (Augé 1995: 79)

Here, the palimpsest, a paper 'which has been written upon twice, the original having been rubbed out' (Onions 1973) or 'prepared for writing on and wiping out again' (Onions 1973), not only provides a model for the relationship of non-place to place, but, in the context of a transitive definition of site, of site-specificity itself. Thus, *Nights In This City* approaches the real city as palimpsest, by acting out a writing over of sites already written upon. Furthermore, in this *moving on* from site, this site-specific performance attempts to define itself *in* the very sites it is caught in the process of erasing.

It is in such contexts that site-specific art frequently works to *trouble* the oppositions between the site and the work. It is in this troubling of oppositions, too, that visual art and architecture's approaches to site realise or may be read through the terms of performance. Reflecting this eclecticism, and the importance of the exchanges between visual art, architecture and theatre in which site-specific work has been defined, this book is organised around a series of thematic points of departure rather than any formal codification of site-specific practice. In considering various approaches to spaces, site, materials, frames, as well as documentation as an instrument of site-specific work, this volume moves across conventionally distinct kinds of practice, ranging from minimalism to land art, contemporary architecture, theatre, happenings, *arte povera*, body art, as well as formally evasive interventions into urban spaces, gallery sites, and even into reading itself. The documentations which intervene into this critical narrative also draw on formally diverse areas of work, just as they make radically differing responses to the paradoxes of presenting site-specific performance to the page. Yet, throughout this work, it is *performance* which returns to define site-specificity, not only as a set of critical terms and as a mode of work, but as a way of characterising *the place* these various site-specific practices reflect upon.

Nights In This City

sheffield 1995/rotterdam 1997

diverse letters and fragments relating to a performance now past
TIM ETCHELLS FOR FORCED ENTERTAINMENT

My love,

In these weeks of making this work we dream constantly of being lost.

"We're off the route... we're off the route..."

Isn't that the definition of liveness in performance? When the thing which began as nothing more than a theatrical act has turned into an event? When guides twitch nervously or appear to be lost? Where safe passage back to the everyday is no longer assured?

Hoping to meet up with you again soon.

Tim

You should start a story with your eyes closed and open them very very slowly. Cities are good places for the beginnings of stories. A story should start with a car pulling away at some traffic lights, or with one light left on in a high rise building at night.

A story should start in a crowded street, or, if that's not possible, it should start in an empty one...

Ladies and gentlemen welcome to Rome... this city is known to me for three things - the beer, the historical buildings and something else... just there, behind these buildings, on the skyline you might just catch a glimpse of the leaning tower of Pisa... and those of you who've been to Venice before will recognise the smell...

Ladies and gentlemen, I think it's fair to warn you that I have been drinking and I've never been that lucky, I mean one night I went out and got punched in the face by a bloke, for no reason, I didn't provoke him or anything... this city, er yeah, this city, let's call it Berlin, Berlin is known for five things, (1) Steel manufacture (2) Football (3) Ray are you sure this is the right route?

We're going to be taking you south on Love Street, past the place where they're thinking of building a new McDonald's, and past the entrance to Knife Walk, so called on account of all the murders that are commonly done there... Ray, watch out for that car, watch out for that car...

All the streets round here got named after famous football hooligans from history and all the buildings got named after ghosts and cleaning products and convicted kerb crawlers... If you look out of the window you might just catch a glimpse of a milkman or a cinema usherette or a drunk or a lawyer... You might just catch a glimpse of a traffic warden in which case you should tell Ray, because he's parked his car on a double yellow, just down there...

This is the place where the soup kitchens used to stand and this is the place where the flood water stopped... and this is the place where a king got killed and this is where someone ran out of a disco crying...

I should warn you ladies and gentlemen that geography's never exactly been my strong suit...

ROTTERDAM

My love,

We are making a guided tour for this city and in trying to determine the route we are helped by many people who live and work here.

We start by asking them questions like: where is the tourist centre of the city, where is a rich neighborhood, where is a poor neighborhood, where is an industrial area?

But these boring questions get the boring answers they probably deserve. We do not find what we are looking for. We switch to another tactic. Richard and Claire are talking to one of our helpers. They ask her:

If you had killed someone and had to dump the body where would you take it?

If you had to say goodbye to a lover where in this city would you most like to do it?

Where in this city might be the best place for a spaceship of aliens to land?

This is what you might call our geography.

Sincerely yours -

Tim

a childhood memory - spending long journeys staring from the car window
and watching the world go by, or of coach journeys
with one's face pressed right against the glass - cars, towns, stories, people, country-
side...

SHEFFIELD

My love,

All night we drive round Sheffield again - trying to find the right route for the bus trip. Afterwards we sit together in a crowded pub and pour over a map already scrawled with notes and abandoned journey plans.

We are at that part of the process where we wish to move or relocate certain districts, build new bridges and tunnels, alter one way systems - all to make the drama of this city's geography suit our purposes. Very funny - if only we could move Attercliffe a little bit closer to the centre of the town, then it would work...

We think of this project like a strange writing onto the city - a playful and poetic reinvention - like you can take the city and project on top of it using words - of course the text contains hardly any facts about the city - it's not an official tour in that sense - it's much more playful. We are driving the streets of Sheffield and pretending that it is Paris.

What's the quote of Baron Munchausen that Terry Gilliam uses in his film? the Baron's motto, or his favourite saying - OUT OF LYING TO THE TRUTH - that could very well be our strategy here.

best wishes -

Tim

Er, I didn't count everyone when we got on the bus so if anyone's not here just stick your hand up... Ray, Ray stick to the route, stick to the route, please stick to the route, I don't know this bit, I don't do this bit, I'm not familiar, Ray please... this is awful... Ray, Ray for old times sake... stick to the route, stick to the route, please please stick to the route, Ray don't do this please Ray please...

Ray... Looking at the map the roads are just wishes for a journey, demanding to be travelled over, red roads, blue rivers.

All the streets round here are named after killers from history and bad politicians, and all the avenues are named after pointless incompetent wars...

All the buildings are named after poisons, and fraudsters and children that died...

Was it in this street that someone had written on a burnt out building, GET WELL SOON??? No. It was... Ray, Ray, I think we're lost Ray...

Ladies and Gentlemen the next stop we're going to make will probably be down near the canal, but for the moment we're headed towards the centre, down this road , past the traffic lights...

All the bridges round here are named after my brothers because we used to throw stones off them. One of them still lives here and the other one has emigrated but they didn't change the name of the bridge...

This street's named after my crazy uncle Pete cos it's got a bend in it and he went round the bend...

A lot of the people you can see from here are ghosts...

ROTTERDAM

My love,
It is ten to eight and we are still struggling to fix the on-board microphone.

What a strange project this is, with its audience and performers inside a bus
- slipping through the centre of its cities and out of control - off the beaten
track, playing always to the differences between on-route and off-route, centre and periphery, with versions of truth both legitimate and illegitimate.

In the end perhaps it is simply a guided tour of the unremarkable, of the
banal made special. The text we've created - pointing out buildings, street
corners, car-parks, patches of wasteground - is always overlaid with other
texts - with the whispered or even shouted texts of other passengers (*"That's
where I used to work...That's the place where..."*) and the silent text of actions
created by those living and working in the city as the bus moves through it.

Sometimes it seems as if all we have to do is gesture to the windows and ask
people to look.

Tim.

SHEFFIELD

My love,
did I say we're writing over the city?

Perhaps I forgot to stress how important it is that the city itself resists this
process. That, where we talk of magic there is simply an ugly dual carriage-
way, that the streets themselves have their own stories, cultures, politics.
There's no authority to what we do - it's all partial, provisional, and often
simply wrong.

In the end the city tells its own story, asks our passengers for theirs, resists or
concurs with the story we are making - all resulting in a complex dialogue,
bringing focus to the different histories written in urban space - the official
historical, the personal, the political, the mythical and the imaginary. How
can these things co-exist? And to whom do they belong? Perhaps those are
our questions.

Tim.

this is where the river ran and this is where the fair was and here, here is where the ferris wheel stood...

and that house was a plague house, and that house was a happy house and that house, that house wasn't there before...

and this is where the singing started and this is where the trail of blood began in earnest...

and this is where the horse bolted and threw the rider to the ground...

This is where the tunnel stopped, and this is where the race ended, and this is where the trains used to start their journeys to places far off and this is where the glass of milk got spilled...

All this used to be mud and before that it was sand...

And this is where the army halted and where a lawyer served a writ and this, this is a place of betrayals...

Coming down through the universe and closing in on here.

Spaces

I would like the happening to be arranged in such a way that
I could at least see through the happening to something that
wasn't it.

(Cage in Kostalanetz 1980: 55)

In relation to minimalism, as Douglas Crimp and Michael Fried's analyses suggest, site-specificity is linked to the incursion of 'surrounding' space, 'literal' space or 'real' space into the viewer's experience of the artwork. In posing questions of the location or 'place' of the object, minimalism's interventions into the gallery engaged with the different orders of space in which the sculptural work is defined, undermining conventional oppositions between the virtual space of the artwork and the 'real spaces' of its contexts. Indeed, this address to inter-related orders of space, in which the viewer's privileged position as reader 'outside' the work is challenged, has played a key part not only in minimalism's site-specificity, but in the addresses to site and the performance of place in visual art, architecture and site-specific theatre. In this context, minimalism's exploration of the viewer's engagement with site in the 'White Cube' gallery (O'Docherty 1986) provides a key point of departure from which to elaborate a range of site-specific interventions into the gallery, the city, and other 'found' sites, which, although operating through a variety of disciplines and means, each take their effect *in performance*.

Performing the Gallery: Robert Morris and Michelangelo Pistoletto

In placing mirrored surfaces on to the unitary forms which he had introduced in the early 1960s, the artist Robert Morris radically extended his address to the viewer's encounter with the inter-related spaces in which the work is defined. Whereas Morris' unitary forms, such as *Untitled* (1966), a painted plywood box 48 inches high and 96 inches deep and wide, seemed to translate the interior white walls of the 'White Cube' gallery space (O'Docherty 1986) on to the exterior surfaces of a sculptural work, *untitled (Mirrored Cubes)* (1965) allows the spaces of the gallery to penetrate 'into' the object, as if to abolish the visual integrity of the sculptural work in favour of its site.

As Morris himself pointed out in the first of his published 'Notes on Sculpture' of 1966, however, with regard to the unitary forms, 'simplicity of shape does not necessarily equate with simplicity of experience' (Morris 1993: 8). Indeed, Morris conceived of this '[s]o-called Minimal art' (Morris 1993d: 54) as engaging with real space and real time. Yet here, as elsewhere, Morris introduces the first of a series of apparent contradictions. In his second critical essay, 'Notes on Sculpture, Part 2' of 1966, Morris begins his account of this aesthetic by quoting the sculptor Tony Smith's 'replies to questions about his six-foot steel cube':

> Q: Why didn't you make it larger so that it would loom over the observer?
> A: I was not making a monument.
> Q: Then why didn't you make it smaller so that the observer could see over the top?
> A: I was not making an object.
>
> (Morris 1993a: 11)

Rather than assert the art object's self-containment, the unitary form makes a sculptural intervention into the gallery space, a space which presents itself, textually, as 'empty'. It is a space which, read after the Modernist programme 'to determine the irreducible working essence of art' (Greenberg 1962: 30), the critic Brian O'Docherty characterised as subtracting 'from the artwork all cues that interfere with the fact that it is "art"' where 'the work is isolated from everything that would detract from its own evaluation of itself' (O'Docherty 1986: 14). In this context, Morris' white cubic forms seem to reproduce the gallery's aesthetic, presenting an object evacuated of 'content' which specifically resists the viewer's attempt to read it. Not only does this object resist the reading of textual content, but, as Morris suggests, it is neither large enough to attain monumentality, so as to establish itself as a domi-nating presence in the space, nor small enough to be seen in isolation from its various relationships with the walls and floor, with which, in any case, it is obviously in dialogue. It thus neither offers any set of relationships which might draw and hold attention *within* its terms, nor claims self-containment. In these ways, rather than offer itself as 'a work' to be 'read', Morris' unitary form presents a kind of visual and physical *obstruction*. Yet it is precisely in this event that this form demands that the viewer negotiate bodily with its placement and dimen-sions. Thus, for Morris:

> It was a confrontation with the body. It was the notion that the object recedes in its self-importance. It participates in a complex experience that includes the object, your body, the space, and the time of your experience. It's locked together in these things.
>
> (Morris 1997)

In mimicking the gallery's claim to neutrality and denial of content, the plywood box defers the viewer's attention toward the dynamic oper-ating between herself, the object and the 'empty space' of the gallery, subverting rather than confirming the gallery's late-Modernist aesthetic and ideology. Caught in this deferral, where the conventional distinc-tions between the limits of the sculptural work and its architectural frame are threatened with collapse, the viewer faces not so much a work isolated from interference as the question of *where* attention should be placed.

Through the *untitled (Mirrored Cubes)* first presented in New York in 1965 this address to the spaces of the work and site is brought further forward. Perhaps most obviously, the mirrors complicate the relationship between the object and its context, as if to dissolve the solidity of the unitary form into multiple reflections of the gallery space. In this way, the mirrored cubes might be said to render Morris' gesture transparent. The mirrors present to the viewer the illusion that she is entering 'the space of the work', only to discover that, in looking into this interior, one merely discovers the 'exterior' conditions of this event of looking. Furthermore, the cubes refuse to allow the viewer to relinquish duration, as they produce multiple reflections of each shift of the viewer's perspective or position. Indeed, the mirrors seem to epitomise Morris' attempt to resist the viewer's reading of depth, centre, or internal stability, in an exposure of the contingent character of the unitary form's intervention into the circumstances in which the viewer views.

Yet the mirrors also present contradictions, confusing and playing between different *orders* of space. Despite reflecting the gallery space, and presenting the viewer with the activity and context of her own looking, Morris' organisation of the mirrors as six-sided cubes extends the unitary form's construction of an 'interior' to which the viewer is denied access. Not only does the cube itself assert 'the imperative of the well-built thing' (Morris 1993b: 41), but the organisation of the mirrors across four cubes presented, originally, such that 'the space between the boxes was equal to the combined volume of the 4 boxes' (Compton and Sylvester 1990: 9), reveals a formal logic operating beyond the mirroring function. In his essay 'Anti-Form' of 1968, Morris reflected on the dualistic character of the cubic or rectangular form, observing that '[p]ermuted, progressive, symmetrical organisations have a dualistic character in relation to the matter they distribute. [. . .] The duality is established by the fact that an order, any order, is operating beyond the physical things' (Morris 1993b: 43).

It follows that, while the mirrored cubes appear to confuse the interior space of a work with the exterior circumstances of their presentation, their cubic form creates an 'interior space' to which the mirrors offer only an *illusion* of access. Indeed, these multiple and multiplying reflections are neither properly inside nor outside the cube and, in amplifying the viewer's continually shifting position while re-defining her perception of 'real space', create the illusion of 'interiority' in which the opposition between the 'virtual space' of 'a work' and the 'real space' of the gallery falls into confusion. As a result, the mirrors explicitly open up questions concerning the relationship between fundamentally different but inter-dependent orders of space, in whose opposition the stability and formal identity of the work depends. In his profoundly influential book, *The Production of Space*, the philosopher Henri Lefebvre asks:

> What term should be used to describe the division which keeps the various types of space away from each other [. . .] Distortion? Disjunction? Schism? Break? [. . .] the term used is far less important than the distance that separates 'ideal' space, which has to do with mental (mathematico-logical) categories from 'real' space, which is the space of social practice. In actuality, each of these two kinds of space involves, underpins and presupposes the other.
>
> (Lefebvre 1991: 14)

It is here, at this point of disjunction, that the viewer's effort 'to locate, to place' the sculptural work, is foregrounded. In the case of the unitary forms, in attempting to construct the 'mental space' (Morris 1993c: 176) of the work, the viewer is referred back to her physical occupation of the gallery-space and so to a schism between 'ideal' and 'real' space, as if one might be mapped upon the other. Where the unitary forms acquire mirrored surfaces, the viewer finds herself witnessing her own incursion into a reflected space neither inside nor outside the work, discovering her position at the juncture of spaces which cannot be reconciled one into the other. In both cases, the viewer's acting out of the gallery as *the place for looking* and of the work as that which *should be located* becomes intensely self-reflexive. Indeed, in order to 'objectify' or resolve this process, the viewer must not only delineate the boundaries or limits of a work but separate this work from her own experience of looking. In the context of such 'ventures into the irrationality of actual space', Morris argues, the viewer's attention is inevitably forced toward herself, for:

> Our encounter with objects in space forces us to reflect on our selves, which can never become 'other,' which can never become objects for our external examination. In the domain of real space the subject-object dilemma can never be resolved.
>
> (Morris 1993c: 165)

It follows that where, in the incursion of 'real space', the viewer's experience of the work becomes inseparable from this *acting out*, so this encounter with 'real space' is inextricably linked to a duration measured only in the viewer's reflection upon and awareness of her own activity. In his essay elaborating the phenomenological aspects of installation work, 'The Present Tense of Space' of 1978, Morris emphasised precisely this equation. Noting 'the intimate inseparability of the experience of physical space and that of an ongoing immediate present', he states flatly that 'real space cannot be experienced except in real time' (Morris 1993c: 177–8). Here, then, the *untitled (Mirrored Cubes)* direct the viewer's attention back toward her own effort, in real space and real time, 'to locate, to place' the sculptural work, exposing and articulating the viewer's *performance*.

In contrast to Morris' interventions into an 'empty' or 'evacuated' space, Michelangelo Pistoletto's later installations explore the complex role of anticipation and memory, as well as present experience, in the 'writing over' of the 'real spaces' of the gallery. A principal proponent and shaping influence of the *arte povera* movement emerging in Turin, Milan and subsequently Rome in 1966 and 1967, Pistoletto substantially developed his work in the 1960s and 1970s through explorations of real space in installations employing mirrors and Plexiglas. Taking as his point of departure notions of the present tense of real space, Pistoletto's first mirror pictures articulated spatial disjunctions through the presence of the figure. First realised in *Il Presente* (*The Present*) of 1961, in which the life-size image of a male spectator facing away from the viewer is laid over the surface of a mirror leant against the gallery wall, the mirror picture effects a convergence of incompatible spaces. Producing, the critic Bruno Cora argues, a 'relationship of instantaneousness between the painted figure, the viewer of the painting, and his or her reflection in it' (Cora 1995: 43), this 'picture' creates the scene for a series of intrusions: for the 'virtual' and 'real' viewers' mutual occupation of and displacement from each other's spaces. Subject, Pistoletto suggests, to 'a perpetual present movement' (Cora 1995: 43), the mirror picture is constituted in this spatial disjunction, where, subject to duration and the viewer's performance, virtual and real spaces are seen to be written over each other.

In *LE STANZE* (*THE ROOMS*), twelve consecutive installations occupying the spaces of the Christian Stein Gallery in Turin from October 1975 to September 1976, Pistoletto presented the mirror, for the first time, without intervention on to its surface, in a further articulation of the complex overlaying of virtual and real spaces. Exposing the conditions in and under which a work is always in the process of being anticipated, produced and remembered, where 'real space' is subject to being 'written over' by experience and imagination, Pistoletto traces out a series of complex relationships between the real and virtual spaces of the rooms and their various reflections. In the first of these relationships, Pistoletto's mirror, as a surface which articulates the interdependency of real and virtual spaces, occupies a series of real doorways in the gallery whose dimensions coincide with those of the mirror pictures. The rooms of the Stein gallery, Pistoletto notes in writing of the first installation, 'open directly into one another, along the same axis. The dimensions of one of the "doorways" are those of my mirror pictures (125 × 230 cms) and thus I imagined a mirror surface placed on the wall of the end room.'

In this context, the twelve successive exhibitions proceed to mark a rhythmic passage of time, introducing anticipation and memory into the experience of both the 'real rooms' and the work of 'writing over' them. Indeed, just as the virtual spaces of the work write over the 'real space' of the room, so this process in time is an instrument by which Pistoletto's installations anticipate, remember and so write over each other. Yet, in this work, each writing over, in space, time or imagination, is characterised by the attempt to recover the real rooms. Paradoxically, of course, and after representation's relationship with its object, or de Certeau's account of the 'symbolic (named)', the 'real rooms' can only be recovered as the antithesis of this writing over, as that which *becomes absent* in the very spaces of the imagined, anticipated or remembered rooms.

In this sense, as the instrument in which the real rooms, and this process, are remembered, Pistoletto's documentation of *LE STANZE* is *no less* the work than any other moment in this passage of time away from their 'real spaces'. Reflecting, in *THE ROOMS, SECOND PART*, on the installation, in the 'real rooms', of a full-size photograph of the first exhibition, Pistoletto observes that in this recording 'the mirror has thus been "trapped" by the camera, which has forced it to reproduce *THE ROOMS* in definite form; that the real rooms have become virtual, in that they have become shut off behind their own photograph'. Yet, paradoxically, Pistoletto proposes that in this very loss may lie the key to the real spaces from which this record departs, for 'the impact with the present flatness of the subject (which we were previously able to enter and to explore halfway) makes us perhaps more sensitive to the previous experience'. In this process, 'documentation', in so far as it 'writes over' and yet is *seen through*, acts as a form of palimpsest. Thus, with regard to the second installation's *representation* of the first, Pistoletto concludes, 'in "overturning" a medium to serve creative expression, it not only becomes useful, but also declares its limits, its fragility, its precariousness'.

Through *LE STANZE* Pistoletto addresses a paradox that Morris also reflects upon: that real space and virtual space are defined only *in* each other. Here, real space must be approached in its *absence*, at the limit or disruption of the work's virtual spaces, for to 'conceptualise' real space is precisely to 'write over it'. It is in this context that Morris and Pistoletto's work seeks to provoke a double awareness through the viewer's mapping of one space over another. Like Morris' interventions, Pistoletto's work, then, articulates this inter-dependency, challenging the viewer's privileged position 'outside' these relationships. Rather than permit the construction of a perspective within which the work finds its place, these interventions position the viewer at the disjunction of spaces, where the work and its sites are in the process of being acted out. Furthermore, as Pistoletto's approach to *THE ROOMS* suggests, this disjunction between 'real' and 'virtual' spaces also operates outside the gallery, providing the basis of a broader consideration of place and space.

Performing the City: Krzysztof Wodiczko

In contrast to the 'White Cube' gallery's signification of *emptiness*, the urban landscape offers a profusion and complexity of signs and spaces where the 'condition of reception' Crimp first identifies with site-specificity might be countered by an *excess* of information. Yet, although the city offers a text which is evidently very different to that into which the minimalist object intervenes, approaches to the city as site may still operate in the disjunctions between spaces, arising where the distinctions between spaces in which a work might establish its parameters are called into question.

Through his large-scale public projections, the émigré Polish artist Krzysztof Wodiczko works to expose the ideological complexities which underlie everyday readings and experiences of the city. Assuming that the built environment functions as a signifying system whose meanings can be destabilised, Wodiczko projects appropriated media-images of the body which, he suggests, are 'already carved into the memory

of the viewers' (Wodiczko and Ferguson 1992: 48), on to specific buildings in order to reveal the languages of power and authority operating
within the cityscape. Projecting images which might 'pervert or act as
a parasite' (Wodiczko and Ferguson 1992: 62) on the buildings they
illuminate, Wodiczko's interventions work to challenge and displace
the architectural, ideological and visual languages he works through and
on. In this sense, Wodiczko's strategy is overtly deconstructive and
aligned with the 'post-modern' tactics of picture-theory artists such as
Sherry Levine, Cindy Sherman, Barbara Kruger, Louise Lawler and
Jenny Holzer. Yet where these artists' work exposes the instability of
the pictorial and linguistic systems in which they are constituted,
Wodiczko's points of departure are analyses of architecture and space
as loci of power and authority. In *The Production of Space* Henri Lefebvre
outlines an understanding of the function of the city's monuments which
seems to underpin Wodiczko's position, stating that:

> Monumentality [. . .] always embodies and imposes a clearly
> intelligible message. It says what it wishes to say – yet it hides a
> good deal more: being political, military, and ultimately fascist in
> character, monumental buildings mask the will to power and the
> arbitrariness of power beneath signs and surfaces which claim to
> express collective will and collective thought.
>
> (Lefebvre 1991: 143)

It is precisely against this masking function that Wodiczko's practice is
directed. Inscribing on to the monument that which it hides or silences,
Wodiczko unveils the complexity of its architectural, ideological or
political subtexts, complicating a reading of the city's signs. His projections, he suggests, serve to expose 'meaningful silences which must be
read. My projections are attempts to carve those silences into the monuments and spaces which propagate civic and dramatic fictions within
the social sphere' (Wodiczko and Ferguson 1992: 51–2).

For Ewa Lajer-Burcharth, writing of Wodiczko's 'brilliantly illumi-
nated projection of a human hand' on to the AT&T building, New

York, in November 1984, in advance of Ronald Reagan's second inaugural speech, the superimposition of this 'common and recognizable gesture of the American political ritual: the pledge of allegiance' on to an overt symbol of corporate power 'suggested that these disparate elements are part of the same body, signs in the same political spectacle' (Lajer-Burcharth 1987: 147). In graphically exposing this building's assertion of presence and power by projecting upon it 'images in which the media present people like buildings' (Wodiczko and Ferguson 1992: 51), Wodiczko produces a disjunctive relationship between the anthropomorphism of the built monument and the monumental function of this iconic image. Thus, Lajer-Burcharth argues, while asserting 'architecture's involvement in the maintenance of a certain order' (Lajer-Burcharth 1987: 147), the AT&T projection has the effect of 'introducing a foreign element into the original structure', as a consequence of which

> the spectator was left uncertain as to the naturalness of this new
> 'body.' The effect of interruption and ambiguity extended to the
> homogenous, bureaucratic cityscape of downtown Manhattan,
> where the fissured AT&T building suddenly struck a dissonant
> note [disturbing] that visual unity on which the function of the
> city as spectacle depends.
>
> (Lajer-Burcharth 1987: 148)

Such uncertainty is fundamental to the character of Wodiczko's procedures. Reproduced in such a way that they 'will have certain structural qualities of the monument in order to make an organic counter-connection' (Wodiczko and Ferguson 1992: 50), Wodiczko's projections work to revive the very monuments they seek to disturb. Paradoxically, Wodiczko emphasises, by illuminating the monument, 'no matter what I project, no matter how critical I want to be, I bring it to its former glory, its presence' (Wodiczko and Ferguson 1992: 62). Indeed, these projections not only rely on a recuperation of the monuments they critique, but valorise the 'monumental function' of the media images through which this recuperation is effected. Commenting on his projection of the caterpillar tracks and engine of a tank, immediately below the image of a pair of hands caught in a gesture of hiding or masking, on to the plinth of the Duke of York Column, near Admiralty Arch in central London in 1985, Wodiczko stressed that his projections 'are not critical images, as you can see, they just belong to a different repertoire of iconography', where, in the event of seeing one 'myth' through another 'there is the possibility of challenging both' (Wodiczko 1986).

Indeed, in grafting these appropriated 'media-images' of the body on to the 'official body' of the architectural façade (Wodiczko and Ferguson 1992: 51), Wodiczko's projections challenge the distinction between the 'built monument' and the 'projected image' by resolving the cityscape into a play of representations. It is in this context that Rosalyn Deutsche proposes, in her essay 'Architecture of the Evicted', that the concept of 'projection' in Wodiczko's work is best understood in terms of 'the procedural dimension of language', concluding that in 'calling attention to and manipulating architecture's language', Wodiczko's interventions reveal themselves to be 'projections on to projections' (Deutsche 1996: 31). Wodiczko has similarly invited a reading of his practice in terms of the intervention of one semiotic system into another, observing that 'photography, architecture, planning, advertising, painting, sculpture, film and television rely on existing codes. So, for me, there isn't a big difference in the end between the monument and the projected image' (Wodiczko and Ferguson 1992: 50).

This conflation of the functioning of art, architecture and these projected images also suggests that, in rendering the built environment as projections, Wodiczko's practices themselves become *part of* the city. Rather than establish a vantage point from which the city's 'text' might be read, or constituting a work explicitly 'other' to the cityscape, Wodiczko's ephemeral inscriptions produce 'a counter-image or counter-monument' (Wodiczko and Ferguson 1992: 50) which participates in the cityscape. Wodiczko states flatly that: 'In order to understand a public projection it must be recorded and announced as any significant urban event is. Events that project themselves on the city, even if they take place outside of it, are part of the experience of the city' (Wodiczko 1992: 196).

In being recorded and announced as an urban event, the projections function not only *in* the built environment, but are absorbed back into the media to become yet another repertoire of iconography in which the city's meanings are produced. Indeed, it is in this context that Wodiczko's work most obviously asserts the continuities between the eighteenth-century monument, the International Style corporate skyscraper and appropriated media-images, as these projections reveal, participate in, and become subject to, the signifying systems in which the city is continually being reproduced and so defined.

Such a participation in the cityscape, however, does not mean that Wodiczko's practices are simply absorbed back into the monumental function of the architecture and images they inhabit. In effecting a 'mobilisation of monuments' (Wodiczko 1996: 55), inherited and contemporary, one against the other, Wodiczko explicitly works *in excess* of the monumental function of the images he deploys and addresses. Engaging in strategies which Ewa Lajer-Burcharth characterises as 'visual disarticulation' (Lajer-Burcharth 1987: 148) where the languages he appropriates turn back against themselves, Wodiczko understands his projections to effect 'a disruption of a routine and passive percep-tion of the ideological theatre of the built environment as well as a disruption of our imaginary place in it' (Wodiczko 1996: 55). Indeed, as Wodiczko implies, although effected through semiotic systems, these interventions are not limited in a simple way to a disruption of *reading*. In *The Production of Space*, and posing the question, 'Does it make sense to speak of a "reading" of space?', Lefebvre asserts that while both 'natural and urban spaces are, if anything, "over-inscribed" [. . .] what one encounters here are directions – multifarious and overlapping instructions' (Lefebvre 1991: 142). He goes on to state, more categor-ically, that:

> Space lays down the law because it implies a certain order – and hence also a certain disorder [. . .] Space commands bodies, prescribing or proscribing gestures, routes and distances to be covered [. . .] The 'reading' of space is thus merely a secondary and practically irrelevant upshot, a rather superfluous reward to the individual for blind, spontaneous and *lived* obedience.
>
> (Lefebvre 1991: 143)

Indeed, as de Certeau tells us, the city does not function only as a text, even as it operates as a signifying system. Like de Certeau's street plan, architecture, in its various operations, constitutes a 'place' realised in the multiple and diverse practices of its users. It follows that Wodiczko's interventions must be located not simply in terms of *reading*, but in this very diversity of spatial practices: according to the 'pedestrian', the 'walker', in relation to this 'lived obedience'. It is here, too, that the significance of these projections' participation in the city becomes clearer.

In calling into question architecture's syntax, these counter-monuments not only complicate a reading of the city's signs, but create their own place, realised in a certain momentary disordering and disruption of the monument's authority. In this context, these projections' 'visual disarticulation', their disruption of architecture's *place*, is realised in spatial practices which subvert the monument's capacity to order, to 'command bodies'. Reflecting on the deconstructive effect of these superimpositions, Wodiczko emphasises that: 'My art must be understood, then, as a form of aesthetic politics; of making space within the space of political art (polis) [. . .] my art, as politics, may then de-politicize this totally political art – this monument' (Wodiczko and Ferguson 1992: 63–4).

Furthermore, in Wodiczko's equation between the body and the built environment, this disordering or disruption of the monument's place has a further and immediate effect for the user. Arguing, with reference to Michel Foucault, that 'our position in society is structured through bodily experience with architecture' (Wodiczko 1992: 199),

Wodiczko's counter-monument works to reveal and so confront the reader with the body as the *hidden text* of the city's construction. In approaching a building, he emphasises that:

> I complete the body (the architectural form) after I learn what that body can do, what the ability of the body to speak is. This is a kind of phenomenological investigation [. . .] I need to assign speech to each part of a particular building so that it will be able to speak in my terms, to speak in a more specific way than it already does.
>
> (Wodiczko 1992: 198)

In enacting the body as the site of the city's construction, Wodiczko assumes and addresses an intimate connection between the city's signs of the body and the construction of bodily experience. Thus, in animating this *textual* address to architecture's articulation of and effect upon the subject, these projections attempt to provoke a *bodily* confrontation with architecture. Through these large image projections, Wodiczko suggests: 'You can really match part of the body with part of the building, something that is hard to imagine without seeing it [. . .] It's possible to see projected images as though they were projected from inside the body out, onto the building' (Wodiczko 1992: 202).

In this moment, Wodiczko's projections *work over* the disjunction between the city as text and as lived experience, and so the disjunction between the reading of 'ideal [. . .] mental (mathematico-logical) categories' of space and the experience of 'real space [. . .] the space of social practice' (Lefebvre 1991: 14). In doing so, Wodiczko calls into question the limits of his own artwork, the city as site, and the viewer's bodily confrontation with the building in order to reveal their construction in each other. It is here, too, that these counter-monuments' *disordering* of architecture's place addresses the individual's experience of the city and, through this, the construction of the individual in its spaces. Wodiczko emphasises that:

My work attempts to enter and trespass this field of vision; the position of the individual as subject being constructed, or produced through the urban space in relation to others and in relation to monuments. I try to disrupt this continuous process of reproducing the individual in space.

(Wodiczko and Ferguson 1992: 64)

Rather than effect a series of deconstructive moves upon the city's semiotic systems, Wodiczko's work addresses the city's architecture as a place which the individual realises in spatial practices, and through which she herself is realised. Treating architecture as this practiced place, Wodiczko's counter-monuments disrupt its 'orderly' performance, effecting a 'de-regulation' of the spatial practices in which the city's monuments are realised. Confronted, in this way, with architecture's displacement, Wodiczko notes:

People speak with each other in front of this dialogue. People remember what they have seen, and what they have discussed, and with whom they discussed it [. . .] When it is all remembered in this way, the Projection will stay, and the projected image will be seen as missing.

(Wodiczko 1996: 56)

Finally, Wodiczko's work comes to define 'its' place in these dislocations, allowing its own spaces to remain elusive, realised in events and practices which *counter* the monument's authority and control rather than establish any separate identity. In this sense, Wodiczko's projections obtain a specificity to site by producing a kind of negative space, or lacuna, where the 'pedestrian' becomes aware of her own performance *in* and *of* the city.

Where Wodiczko's projections, in coming to the performance of 'real' space through the viewer's reading of the city's text, might seem antithetical to Morris' and Pistoletto's response to the 'deprived space' (Tschumi 1994: 42) of the 'White Cube' gallery, in fact both these strategies approach 'site' by *working over* the disjunction between the reading of space and the experience of space. In blurring the distinctions between the virtual space of a work and the real spaces in which the viewer acts, these strategies expose the performance of the places into which they intervene. Yet it is in contemporary architectural theory and practice, acting under the influence of both post-minimal explorations of the phenomenology of space and contemporary theories of the text, that this disjunction between 'spaces' is articulated most clearly.

Architecture and Event: Bernard Tschumi

In locating his definition of architecture in what he argues is the most intractable of its 'internal contradictions', the fact that, by 'its very nature', architecture is 'about two mutually exclusive terms – space and its use or, in a more theoretical sense, the concept of space and the experience of space' (Tschumi 1994: 15–16), Bernard Tschumi's various theoretical and built projects have treated the 'disjunction' which Henri Lefebvre describes as an inherent part of architecture's operation. Indeed, in his first substantive theoretical essay, 'The Architectural Paradox' of 1975, Tschumi argued that the experience of architecture is constituted in the very gap 'between ideal space (the product of mental processes) and real space (the product of social practice)' (Tschumi 1994a: 31).

In this context, Tschumi has gone on to read not only Modernist architectural practice, in its aspiration to a 'universally valid geometrical form' (Klotz 1988: 421), its emphasis on structural truth, utility and functionalism, but also the subsequent post-modern eclectic recuperation of styles, genres and conventions from the past (Jencks 1987) as attempts to evade this disjunction through a retreat into form. Concluding that 'architecture is not a matter of style and cannot be reduced to a language' (Tschumi 1994: 3), Tschumi aligns Modern and post-modern projects in architecture with Modernist painting's aspirations to 'foundation' (Kaye 1994) and so to attempts to overcome the instability of the 'sign' through an appeal to the 'well-defined signified that guarantees the authenticity of the work of art' (Tschumi 1987: VII).

As this analysis suggests, Tschumi's work provides for a reading of post-structuralist theories of the text, including 'the research of limits, the practice of intertextuality, and the crisis of the sign' (Martin 1990: 1) into architectural theory and practice. Indeed, in the *Cinegram Folie* (Tschumi 1987), detailing the planning of his first built project, Le Parc de La Villette, developed in Paris from 1983 to 1998, Tschumi specifically aligned his work with Jacques Derrida's deconstructive practices. Here, he emphasises, while La Villette plainly rejected Modernist aesthetics, more fundamentally 'the project takes issue with a particular premise of architecture, namely, its obsession with *presence*, with the idea of a meaning immanent in architectural structures and forms which directs its signifying capacity' (Tschumi 1987: VII).

In describing architecture in terms of this disjunction, then, Tschumi's work has engaged not only with radical architectural thought, but literary criticism, the picture-theory art to which Wodiczko's work is linked, as well as 'performance, photography, cinema, etc.'(Tschumi 1985: 23). While drawing on the work of artists and theorists emphasising post-structuralist concepts of the sign and the text (Tschumi 1985: 24), Tschumi has also defined his practice in relation to the work of 'early "concept-performance" artists' and their emphasis upon the phenomenology of space. Thus, in 'The Architectural Paradox', Tschumi positioned his work in relation to the post-minimal installation art of Bruce Nauman, Doug Wheeler, Robert Irwin, and Michael Asher, where:

> By restricting visual and physical perception to the faintest of all stimulations, they turn the expected experience of the space into something altogether different. The almost totally removed sensory definition inevitably throws the viewers back on

themselves. In 'deprived space' [. . .] the materiality of the body coincides with the materiality of space [and] the subjects only 'experience their own experience'.

(Tschumi 1994a: 41–2)

In making these references, however, Tschumi always refers back to the disjunctive relationship between the concept and experience of space. In this context, it is the post-structuralist critique of the stability of the sign that finally confirms, for Tschumi, not only the nature of this disjunction but, ironically, that architecture cannot be reduced to a text. In 'The Architectural Paradox' Tschumi repeatedly emphasises the opposition between real and ideal space. Yet, in a key passage echoing Lefebvre's qualification that in actuality, 'each of these two kinds of space involves, underpins and presupposes the other' (Lefebvre 1991: 14), Tschumi relates this opposition to the functioning of the sign. Arguing that 'architecture is made of two terms that are interdependent but mutually exclusive', he concludes:

> *architecture constitutes the reality of experience while this reality gets in the way of the overall vision. Architecture constitutes the abstraction of absolute truth, while this very truth gets in the way of feeling.* We cannot both experience and think that we experience. 'The concept of dog does not bark'; the concept of space is not in space.

(Tschumi 1994a: 48)

Tschumi's statement that '"The concept of dog does not bark"; the concept of space is not in space' draws on his own conversations with Lefebvre, in which Lefebvre quotes Spinoza's well-known dictum concerning the relation of language to the world. In the context of post-structuralist theory, however, this distinction refers, most clearly, to the relationship of the signified to the referent under Ferdinand de Saussure's rules of structural linguistics. Proposing that the constitution of the sign in the relationship between signifier (the mark or sound 'dog', for example) and signified (the 'unit of meaning': the 'concept of dog') is determined entirely through the arbitrary rules of a linguistic system, Saussure set out an understanding of language as a conventional construction always complete in itself. Furthermore, in the context of language's self-regulation, the dog which barks (the referent) plays no part in the production of meaning. Indeed, it is the joining of signifier and signified that, in making manifest the very 'concept of dog', is the pre-condition to any *thinking* of the referent. As a result, the sign and its referent are in a relationship of absolute and unbreachable, if paradoxical, difference: the 'concept of space' is necessarily *other* to space; 'the concept of dog does not bark'.

It follows that, where, '[e]tymologically, to define space means both "to make space distinct" and "to state the precise nature of space"' (Tschumi 1994a: 30), the very nature of the sign introduces a schism into architecture's definition. In so far as architecture's referent is 'space', then architecture's signifying capacity, its ability to state the precise nature of space, necessarily manifests itself as *other* to its 'making of space distinct', even as it permits a thinking of 'felt space'. Indeed, here, architecture's definition of space becomes inseparable from the oppositions between the thought and the felt, concept and experience, signified and referent. Yet these oppositions do not, in themselves, properly characterise the interdependence of 'ideal' space and 'real' space to which Tschumi refers, or, for that matter, provide the basis for a deconstructive practice. Indeed, it is precisely in the de-stabilising of such binary oppositions that deconstruction is conventionally defined (Benjamin 1988: 10). Moreover, arising as part of his critique of the metaphysics of presence, Derrida reveals his own deconstructive practices in an upsetting of Saussure's description of the opposition between signifier and signified.

In his description of the rules of structural linguistics, Saussure describes the functioning of language as a self-contained, self-regulating system through which meaning becomes *present*. However, within Saussure's own terms, this claim can be read as resting on a contradiction. Within the self-regulated system Saussure proposes, the functioning of the signifier, its ability to join with the signified, is dependent not upon what the signifier *is* but upon *what it is not*. Indeed, the very self-containment of the system requires that the signifier be recognised, and so defined by the reader, in its relation of difference with all other signifiers. This means that, in so far as he claims that in the joining of signifier and signified meaning becomes present, Saussure can be accused of supposing that there is a realm of the signified, of 'concepts', somehow existing beyond the functioning of the signifier. Only by gaining access to such a realm could the play of difference, by which the signifier functions, result in the presence of meaning. Yet any such realm would both precede and exist beyond the self-contained, self-regulating linguistic structure.

To question the opposition of signifier and signified which Saussure assumes, however, is to doubt the very decidability of meaning under the rules of structural linguistics. If the signified is not a function of presence but, like the signifier, of absence and difference, then it follows that meaning becomes subject to the same processes of differentiation which permits the functioning of the signifier. Meaning becomes, like the signifier, not a function of *what it is*, but of *what it is not*. Indeed, where, as Derrida argues, 'the signified always already functions as signifier' (Derrida 1974: 7), meaning can never be present, for the move toward the signified finds itself caught in the endless play of 'difference' and so 'deferral'; always subject to *différance*.

It is in this context that the interdependence of real space and ideal space, as Tschumi refers to it, might be properly understood. Under Derrida's critique of the 'transcendental signified', the sign is unstable and incomplete, always subject to undecidability. It follows that architecture's definition of space is paradoxical, for, as a text, as a signifying system, architecture cannot state the precise nature of space, and yet architecture's 'making of space distinct' cannot be thought without such a text. It follows that architecture's definition of space actually operates *in* this very relation between real space and ideal space, where the 'real' is defined by, but cannot rest in, the terms of the 'ideal', while the 'ideal' is unable to *state* the precise nature of that which is *made*

distinct. As a consequence, and like the sign itself, architecture's definition of space is always in deferral, it is inescapably restless. Thus,
Tschumi argues:

> The concept of disjunction is incompatible with a static,
> autonomous, structural view of architecture. But it is not anti-
> autonomy or anti-structure; it simply implies constant,
> mechanical operations that systematically produce dissociation
> (Derrida would call it *differance*) in space and time, where an
> architectural element only functions by colliding with a
> programmatic element.
>
> (Tschumi 1988: 35)

It is then this effect of dissociation, or 'differance', which properly
describes the operation of architecture's definition of space. It is in this
context, too, that Tschumi seeks to define his architectural practice
not simply with respect to the opposition between ideal and real space,
but in its deconstruction. Thus Tschumi looks toward an architecture
which works to reveal, and exacerbate, this instability; which postpones
or disturbs architecture's *ability to rest* in its definition of space and so
assert foundation or finality. In this sense, too, Tschumi's notion of a
deconstruction in architecture has nothing to do with the post-modern
attitude toward style and convention, for it cannot be resolved into a
form or style, but addresses, as Derrida suggests, the 'architecture of
architecture', or architecture's very organisation of knowledge: 'the
assumption that *architecture must have a meaning*, it must *present* it and,
through it, *signify*' (Derrida 1985: 9).

This address to architecture's definition of space reflects directly on
notions of site and site-specificity. Site-specificity, in this context, might
best be thought of as occurring in a working over of this relationship,
as a *restlessness* arising in an upsetting of the opposition between 'ideal'
and 'real' space, in precisely the manner of Morris', Pistoletto's, and
Wodiczko's interventions. Furthermore, in upsetting or deconstructing
these oppositions, site-specificity is intimately tied to notions of event

and performance. In this context, and by way of a model of connections between architecture and performance, Tschumi's first built project provides for just such an approach to both space and site.

For Le Parc de La Villette, an 'Urban Park for the twenty-first Century' (Tschumi 1987: II), Tschumi was charged with developing a 125-acre site on the northeast side of Paris containing a pre-existing Museum of Science and Industry, a City of Music, and a Grande Halle for exhibitions and concerts. Here, he proposed, the relationship between architecture and its 'use' must embrace diverse purposes and functions. Thus, in rejecting the imposition of 'a masterly construction' (Tschumi 1987: IV), a compliment to the pre-existing structures, or a deconstruction of previous architectural definitions of the site, Tschumi sought to deploy an 'abstract mediation' between the site and the project's 'programme' or 'list of required utilities' (Tschumi 1994c: 112). In doing so, Tschumi's focus falls on disjunctive and multiple relations between the built environment and its uses: above all, he argues, 'the project directed an attack against cause and effect relationships, whether between form and function, structure and economics or (of course) form and programme' (Tschumi 1987: VII).

To this end, Tschumi's design does not determine a single or unified abstract structure which might regulate a series of specific and limited uses, but seeks to effect 'a radical questioning of the concept of structure' through 'the superimposition of three autonomous (and coherent) structures' (Tschumi 1985: 3). Thus, opposing 'the ascendancy of any privileged system or organizing element' (Tschumi 1987: VI), Tschumi orchestrates the overlaying of a structure of 'surfaces' ('the system of spaces'), 'lines' ('the system of movements') and 'points' ('the system of objects') (Tschumi 1987: 5) in whose interaction he seeks 'to dislocate and de-regulate' rather than establish La Villette's 'meaning' (Tschumi 1987: VII).

While the system of surfaces is defined by its prospective programmatic needs, providing specific architectural forms for 'play, games, body exercises, mass entertainment, markets, etc.', the system of lines provides for 'high density pedestrian movement' qualified by two co-ordinate axes or covered galleries running the length and breadth of the site, for alleys of trees linking key activities and a 'cinematic promenade of gardens' (Tschumi 1987: 8). Ruled by a 'strategy of differences', the gardens offer a series of 'spaces for the interventions' (Tschumi 1987: 8) of artists, designers and architects. Finally, the system of points is created by 'exploding programmatic requirements throughout the site', in the form of built *Folies*, or 'points of intensity' (Tschumi 1987: 4). Constructed as variations on a 'basic $10 \times 10 \times 10$ metre cube or a three-storey construction of neutral space' (Tschumi 1987: 7) and distributed according to 'a point-grid coordinate system at 120-metre intervals' (Tschumi 1987: 7), the *Folies* might be adopted for different, even conflicting, uses at different times. It is this system of 'points', and the functioning of the *Folies*, that can be read as providing keys to an understanding of the effect of Tschumi's strategies.

Indicating, in its original eighteenth-century use, 'an extravagant house of entertainment', the *Folie* refers, in French, also to madness or insanity. Yet, while Tschumi warns that the *Folie's* psychoanalytical meaning can be related 'to its built sense – folly – only with extreme caution' (Tschumi 1987: 16), La Villette implies a kind of programmatic 'madness', where the distribution of the *Folies* without regard to the conflicting logics of the two other autonomous systems provides focal points for 'the combination of incompatible activities (the running track passes through the piano bar inside the tropical greenhouse)' (Tschumi 1987: 4). Acting, through their repetition, as 'a common denominator' for the Park, and built as a series of deviations from a given architectural 'primary structure' or 'original norm', the *Folie* is defined, *programmatically*, as a point of intensity which, through its *use*, will be continually 'constituting itself as a system of relations between objects, events, and people' (Tschumi 1987: 24). Indeed, in this context, Tschumi likens La Villette's fragmentation to that of 'the contemporary city and its many parts', which, by analogy, might be 'made to correspond with the dissociated elements of schizophrenia' (Tschumi 1987: 17). Here, in their continual redefinition through conflicting *uses*, the *Folies* at once intensify this dissociation and provide points of temporary resolution.

In this respect, too, the *Folies* allude to La Villette's basic operation. If, as Tschumi suggests, 'madness articulates something that is often negated in order to preserve a fragile cultural or social order' (Tschumi 1987: 17), then 'madness' might also provide the metaphor for the effect of the Park. In the combination of these distinct systems, Tschumi argues, 'the Park became architecture against itself: a dis-integration' (Tschumi 1987: VII), for, '[t]he addition of the systems' internal coherences is not coherent. The excess of rationality is not rational' (Tschumi 1987: VIII).

Indeed, it is through the very rigour of their application that the Park comes to undermine the authority of these structures, 'questioning their conceptual status as ordering machines' (Tschumi 1987: VII). Thus, while the point-grid 'constitutes an absolute rule' for the distribution of the *Folies*, once subject to the conflicting programmatic demands produced by all three systems, it transpires that the grid 'only gives the appearance of order, by simulating it' (Tschumi 1985: 3). Such displacements of the Park's regulatory systems is consistent with Derrida's understanding of the effect of deconstructive practice, where the authority of a structure is brought into question just as it takes its effect. It is a 'displacement', Andrew Benjamin writes, that 'is captured by Derrida when he writes of "norms" being "taken into consideration"; being "reinscribed"; present but no longer in "command". Norms become, in Nietzsche's sense, "fictions"' (Benjamin 1988: 10). In this context the very selection of the grid itself can be read as a tactic intended to produce disjunctions between the Park's formal and programmatic logics. Tschumi observes that the grid

> presented the project team with a series of dynamic oppositions.
> We had to design a park: the grid was anti-nature. We had to
> fulfill a number of functions: the grid was anti-functional.
> We had to be realists: the grid was abstract. We had to respect
> the local context: the grid was anti-contextual. We had to be
> sensitive to site boundaries: the grid was infinite. We had to take
> into account political and economic indetermination: the grid was

determinate. We had to acknowledge the garden precedents: the
grid had no origin.

(Tschumi 1987: VI)

In fact, as this demonstrates, the architectural order of the Park
is not, finally, a formal property of each or any of these systems, but
exists in the tensions between architecture and programme, recalling
the restlessness of architecture's definition of space. Indeed, in this
sense, in imposing conflicting regulatory systems, the Park's formal
authority continually defers to use, creating a topology always being
defined *in practices*. Here, after de Certeau, La Villette might be thought
of as an architecture whose place provokes its own re-ordering, and so
a place which admits of a certain *mobility*. In this sense, Tschumi
proposes, La Villette is not an exercise in 'composition' but in 'the
"*combinative*"', in architecture 'as the object of permutation' (Tschumi
1987: 26).

In this context, not only the form but the meaning of La Villette
becomes evasive. La Villette is openly intertextual, as its systems are
sited in relation to pre-existing architectural systems. Where, Tschumi
argues, the grid's 'serial repetitions and seeming anonymity made it a
paradigmatic twentieth-century form' (Tschumi 1987: VI) associated
with a variety of departures in Modernism, so the red *Folies* make explicit
reference to constructivist design. Yet, Tschumi proposes, these references enter the series of displacements by which the architecture is
constituted, and 'the "truth" of red Folies is not the "truth" of construc-
tivism, just as the "truth" of the system of points is not the "truth" of
the system of lines' (Tschumi 1987: VIII).

Here, La Villette's specific relation to *site* also becomes apparent.
In this sense, La Villette's specificity to site is defined in its *use*, in
the changing and varying practices of its users, and not in any stated
or stable or even probable or predicted relationship. Thus, just as
the grid works toward disjunctive relationships, so, in its approach
to site, Tschumi suggests, 'the Park rejected context, encouraging
intertextuality and the dispersion of meaning. It subverted context:

La Villette is anticontextual. It has no relation to its surroundings. Its plan subverts the very notion of borders on which "context" depends' (Tschumi 1987: VII).

The 'anticontextual' nature of La Villette has to be understood in the disjunction of architecture and its use, however. Defined in opposition to a formal autonomy which would impose itself upon or be oblivious to site, La Villette is anticontextual in the sense of rejecting the stabilities that 'knowing' the context and 'contextualising' assumes. Rather than state the context, La Villette sets conditions for the *performance* of both architecture and site; for its realisation in multiple, diverse and transforming practices. Indeed, in so far as it fosters the play of the signifier, La Villette is an attempt to evade any categorical definition of site, architecture or its use. Thus Tschumi emphasises that La Villette 'aims at an architecture that *means nothing*, an architecture of the signifier rather than the signified – one that is pure trace or play of language' (Tschumi 1987: VIII). Indeed, without *presence* there is no final *location*, only the process or activity of *locating*. Where architecture cannot make an appeal to the transcendental signified, it cannot state or present the site *as* signified, but must defer to the functioning of the signifier. Site-specificity, it follows, is found *in use*; and site, *location*, like architecture itself, is always *being produced*, and so is subject to instability, ephemerality, and temporality. La Villette, then, is an architecture which can be described, after de Certeau, as attempting to catch the 'user' in the act of enunciation, revealing her *acting out* of a perpetually practised place. Site, for Tschumi, is consequently always already subject to the event of location; always already subject to performance, to its realisation in practice. In all these respects, La Villette points back to architecture's *restlessness*. For Tschumi,

> La Villette is a term in constant production, in continuous change, its meaning is never fixed but always deferred, differed, rendered irresolute by the multiplicity of meanings it inscribes. The project aims to unsettle both memory and context, opposing many contextualist and continualist ideals which imply that the

architect's intervention necessarily refers to a typology, origin or determined signified.

(Tschumi 1987: VII–VIII)

If, as Tschumi suggests in 'The Architectural Paradox', 'architecturally, to define space (to make space distinct) literally means "to determine the boundaries"' (Tschumi 1994a: 30), then La Villette operates, again, through a troubling of the *borders* of the work, in a refusal of the clear and stable limit. Thus, in this project, Tschumi provides for an architecture, or set of architectural relations, always *in performance*.

'Placeevent'*: Brith Gof

Since *Goddodin* in 1988, and under the artistic direction of Clifford McLucas and Mike Pearson, the Welsh performance company Brith Gof have created a series of large-scale performances occupying socially and politically charged sites. While *Goddodin*, an epic poem concerning the slaughter of Welsh warriors, was created in collaboration with the industrial percussionists Test Dept. for the disused Rover Car Factory in Cardiff, *Pax*, of 1991–92, was based on a descent of angels and concerned with the environmental plight of the planet, and installed in St David's Hall, Cardiff, the Harland and Wolff shipyard in Glasgow and the British Rail Station in Aberystwyth. Subsequently, *Haearn*, meaning 'iron', was created for the Old British Coal Works in Tredegar, Wales, in 1993 and performed shortly before the building's demolition. *Tri Bywyd* (*Three Lives*), aspects of whose structural complexity can be read against Tschumi's approach to La Villette, was created in 1995 for a rural location near Lampeter in the Welsh county of Ceredigion.

---

* 'Placeevent' is a term taken from correspondence from Clifford McLucas to Nick Kaye, dated 3 June 1996.

Using explicitly 'hybrid' practices, and seeking to provoke a series of dialogues and confrontations between performance and location, Brith Gof construct their site-specific work through exploring unresolved relationships between various channels of address, creating a 'field of activities' (McLucas *et al.* 1995: 17) rather than linear structures. Confronted with multiple, and often interpenetrating narratives and voices, their audiences are invited to encounter the site in which these works are realised as re-framed and overlaid by narratives which challenge and draw on the place of their presentation. Rather than look toward a synthesis of elements through performance, the guiding metaphor for the construction of Brith Gof's work in these places has been the coexistence of distinct 'architectures' inhabiting one another and the site itself without resolution into a synthetic whole. It is a relationship between elements which amplifies a fundamental exchange between site and performance, where, McLucas suggests, the installation of 'ghost' architectures seeks to engage with and activate narratives and properties of a 'host' site. In this context, McLucas observes, the site may offer

> a particular and unavoidable history
> a particular use (a cinema, a slaughterhouse)
> a particular formality (shape, proportion, height, disposition of
>   architectural elements, etc.)
> a particular political, cultural or social context
>
> (Kaye 1996: 213)

Conceiving of their work, Pearson suggests, as 'the latest occupation of a location where occupations are still apparent and cognitively active' (Kaye 1996: 214), these performances are presented as a continuation of their sites' 'use'. Yet, just as these events constitute another inflection of their sites' meanings, so they also define a process in which the *reading of site* is opened up. In these performances, Pearson argues, 'a complex overlaying of *narratives*, historical and contemporary, [creates] a kind of *saturated space*, or scene-of-crime, where [. . .] "everything is potentially important'" (Kaye 1996: 214). Here, the architectural metaphor through which this work is constructed serves to bring a series of thematic, formal, 'found' and built structures into relationship. It is a form, McLucas suggests, which, in *Haearn*, is constructed through the relationship of seven distinct and distinctive 'architectures' each of which operates in a *restless* relationship with its structural partners, as well as the 'architectures' of the 'host' itself. Thus, McLucas emphasises that this piece

> was conceived as a fractured (and incomplete) work. Like Frankenstein's creature, it was constructed from a number of disparate vital organs and parts. Like all ghosts, *Haearn's* body is not solid – the host can be seen through it. The Host and the Ghost, of different origins, are *co-existent* but, crucially, are not *congruent*.
>
> (Kaye 1996: 220)

Here, McLucas suggests, where 'history, location, political and industrial ownership, all resonated through the work' (McLucas, Morgan and Pearson 1995: 48) 'site' is articulated through the installation of architectures reflecting its social, political, and historical location, as well as its formal properties and the bilingualism which defines its cultural contexts. In a 'hybridized piece of work' such as this, McLucas points out, 'there may be 8 or 9 different artforms intermingling with one another. [. . .] Very quickly in a project we have a "field" of things, of activities, and these different fields or architectures might be developed entirely in separation from each other' (McLucas, Morgan and Pearson 1995: 19).

Yet, while this 'field of activities' may produce a formal, thematic and narrative dispersal, McLucas emphasises, each of these means

> somehow activates, or engages with, the narratives of the site [. . .] That might be with its formal architecture, or it might be with the character of the building [. . .] It might be to do with

the history of that building [. . .] the host building [. . .] which
does have personality, history, character, narrative written into it,
into which we put this thing that we've made [. . ..] And between
these two there are transparent architectures, sometimes
supporting each other, sometimes battling against each other.

(McLucas, Morgan and Pearson 1995: 47)

Such approaches to site, Pearson proposes, move 'beyond illustrating
the theme, illustrating the material' (McLucas, Morgan and Pearson
1995: 17) and by 'operating within architectures that are not backdrops'
(McLucas, Morgan and Pearson 1995: 46) open up a reading of performance and site to multiple viewpoints. As a consequence, McLucas
emphasises, in confronting these fractured works, the audience discovers
that 'there's not a single viewpoint [. . .] there's no way to stand outside
it to try and define or divine the material' (McLucas, Morgan and
Pearson 1995: 17).

Rather than present a specific or single *reading* of site, such a fractured work *disperses* the site, constituting 'different groups of audience
in different places' such that 'every single member of the audience is
going to have a different reading of the piece' (McLucas, Morgan
and Pearson 1995: 33). 'Place', in this sense, is explicitly constituted *in
performance itself*, even where the 'site' may have 'a parallel identity' of
its own (CM: McLucas *et al*. 1995: 46), as these interventions activate
and challenge readings of location. Here, McLucas suggests, the site-
specific performance is not simply formally 'hybrid' but is defined, more
directly, where performance and place are invested one in the other.
Thus McLucas stresses that 'the real site-specific works that we do, are
the ones where we create a piece of work which is a hybrid of the place,
the public and the performance' (McLucas, Morgan and Pearson 1995:
48). It is a set of relationships which is fluid, as it remains subject to
the event of its realisation. In these 'truly site-specific pieces of work',
McLucas observes,

There's always a mis-match between the 'host' and the 'ghost',
and from the beginning of the work it's fractured, it's deeply,
deeply fractured [. . .] it actually leads you into techniques which
are of multiple fracture [. . .] we are dealing with a field of
elements, and with symphonic relationships which can sometimes
be made to work, and sometimes can't [. . .] they are more
discursive, and have gaps in them – you can see other things
through.

> (McLucas, Morgan and Pearson 1995: 51)

Consistently with this, in *Tri Bywyd*, rather than present these 'architectures' as a series of interlinked narrative and formal structures,
'architecture' and 'event' are invested one within the other, in 'a hybrid
of architecture and event' where 'a place and what is built there bleed
into each other and constitute another order of existence – something
like "placeevent"' (McLucas 1996). Indeed, this is a strategy which aims
at an *upsetting* of the boundaries of performance and site, and which,
while constituted in these architectures, McLucas emphasises, is a work
which 'exists in real time, in real space' (Kaye 1996: 234).

In his essay 'Architecture and Transgression' of 1976, Bernard
Tschumi envisaged an analogous moment in architecture, where, he
suggests, 'through literal or phenomenal transgression architecture is
seen [. . .] as the momentary and sacrilegious convergence of real space
and ideal space' (Tschumi 1994: 78). It is a moment he identifies with
the 'ultimate pleasure of architecture': 'that impossible moment when
an architectural act, brought to excess, reveals both the traces of reason
and the immediate experience of space' (Tschumi 1994: 89). Here, in
what the architectural critic Anthony Vidler supposes must result in
'the aestheticization of disorder' (Vidler 1988: 19), Tschumi imagines
a synthesis of the experience of space and the concept of space and so
of the 'real' and the 'ideal'. In many ways, site-specific art and performance persistently speculates over such a moment, as it presses toward
the limits of the virtual spaces through which it functions, in an address
to the complexities of *acting out*, while being *subject to*, the 'real spaces'

in which it is defined. In doing so, however, these works also intimate a latent *disorder*, a disorder de Certeau recognised as inherent to the relationship between practice and place, where

> Things *extra* and *other* (details and excesses coming from elsewhere) insert themselves into the accepted framework, the imposed order. One thus has the very relationship between spatial practices and the constructed order. The surface of this order is everywhere punched and torn open by ellipses, drifts, and leaks of meaning: it is a sieve-order.
>
> (de Certeau 1984: 107)

Defined in these relationships between spaces and spatial practices, this site-specific work tests the stability and limits of the very places it *acts out*, at once relying on the order of the sites it so frequently seeks to question or disrupt. In this sense, site-specific art is defined precisely in these ellipses, drifts, and leaks of meaning, through which the artwork and its place may be momentarily articulated one in the other.

Michelangelo Pistoletto

LE STANZE

Ottobre 1975
Settembre 1976

Tau/ma 5

Michelangelo Pistoletto

LE STANZE

Ottobre 1975 – Settembre 1976

Dodici mostre consecutive nell'arco di un anno

alla galleria Christian Stein di Torino

THE ROOMS

October 1975 – September 1976

Twelve consecutive shows in the course of a year

at the Christian Stein Gallery, Turin

Fotografie di Paolo Mussat Sartor

English translation by Malcolm Skey

THE ROOMS

The idea of holding this exhibition came to me on seeing the three rooms of the Stein Gallery in Turin last Spring.

The rooms open directly into one another, along the same central axis. The dimensions of one of the 'doorways' are those of my mirror pictures (125 × 230 cm.) and thus I imagined a mirror surface placed on the wall of the end room, as a virtual continuation of the series of openings from one room into the next.

Until I saw this new gallery, I had never found a reason for exhibiting a mirror surface alone, without any form of intervention on my part. In my mirror pictures there is one aspect which is constant: the relationship between the static image, as fixed by me, and dynamic images of the mirroring process: in the case in point, the static image is pushed right up to the outer edges of the picture, whose perimeter represents the outline of the doorways which precede it physically and which proceed in the reflection.

There are many things I could say about this work; for example, that it cannot be transported elsewhere without relegating it again to the status of a mere mirror; that it 'magnetizes' all the space within the gallery by immobilizing it (by virtue of the fact the gallery immobilizes the mirror for the duration of the exhibition).

I could go on to speak of the spectator, and formulate a hypothesis about the immobility by which he would find himself surrounded (even if he were to move) should he realize that his relationship with the phenomenon is only one of 'registration'.

For his point of view in relation to the picture is immaterial, in that each and every point of the three rooms has been considered in perspective.

The particular point on which I should like to focus attention is the fact that there are three 'doorways' which become seven through reflection.

Only recently scientists discovered the law that all phenomena can be verified in mirror form, except one. Whenever we arrive at a discovery via the instruments of art, it is never microscopic or macroscopic, but always in a *human* dimension.

THE ROOMS, SECOND PART

I have written elsewhere that my mirror pictures cannot be reproduced: that is, they cannot be transformed into another medium, for that would mean the elimination of the dynamic which is their essential aspect. I feel the same is true for this exhibition of THE ROOMS; the only proper medium for its documentation is the living eye which registers it. The spectator moves forward with the light which floods in through and which gets dimmer from room to room.

The experience of the visitors consists in walking up to the mirror (in the furthest and dimmest of the rooms) to find that in it he is almost flat up against the light from the exit he has just entered by: it seems that if he were to take another step forward, he would become as one with the mirror surface, with no body and no reflection.

But the irreproducibility of this experience will emerge with THE ROOMS II, in which the spectator will see the same exhibition as a *reproduction*.

Indeed, through the first doorway (printed life-size in a photograph placed directly over the opening) we see the reproduction of the space we moved through previously.

The observer will note that the mirror has thus been 'trapped' by the camera, which has forced it to reproduce THE ROOMS in definite form; that the real rooms have become virtual, in that they have been shut off behind their own photograph (which thus becomes the only tangible datum); and the impact with the present flatness of the subject (which we were able previously to enter and to explore halfway) makes us perhaps more sensitive to the previous experience.

However, apart from these and other observations and suggestions, I should like to stress a *third* moment, which follows on from the two exhibitions: i.e. publication. For, in deciding to publish the image of the operations, we realize that the same photograph will do equally well for both.

In any piece of research, each single datum is precious.

We should not therefore ignore the fact that in 'overturning' a medium to serve creative expression, it not only becomes useful, but also declares its limits, its fragility, its precariousness.

Since 1964 I have been working with different media, modifying in every case, their conventional use. Each of them, in the course of my research, is made to determine and define the weight and the force of artistic concept. I do not allow my ambition to coincide with the unhesitating acceptance of the idea that the mass media are the message of today.

And this in itself is enough to allow me to use the same media as movers of other messages.

THE ROOMS, NUMBER THREE

Father, son, and creativity

Every man is the son of the son, of the son, of the son, and bears within himself the father of the father, of the father, of the father, of the father.

On the section of wall above each of the doorways which are between the 'Rooms' I have placed first of all the word 'figlio' (son) because it is from the son's point of view that I regard the work. The work realizes itself here, as we have seen, from the very first doorway. The word 'figlio' is repeated above each doorway until the threshold leading beyond the last of the rooms. But this time, the illusion that the mirror reflection simply continues the series of openings and rooms is dispelled, since in the reflection it is the word 'padre' (father) which is repeated from doorway to doorway, from room to room.

The reflection never gives back its own side, but the opposite.

Thus, in virtue of this seventh opening or threshold, which I call the creative point, we are enabled to see our going in and our returning.

But I would add, as far as this exhibition is concerned, that we cannot consider ourselves as entirely 'fathers' until we have walked the entire length of the path of the sons.

THE ROOMS, ACT FOUR

The development of this research inside 'The Rooms' and thus within the twelve programmed exhibitions follows the logic of space, time, and my own presence verifying the effect.

The moment of this writing (4 PM on January 16th 1976) marks the shift from the third to the fourth show, in traditional numerical sequence.

Number three encapsulates the parity of the two (the father and the son) who are reflected in the uneven, central point (the mirror).

Four is even and does not reveal disparity in any way. In Four the central point in which the opposing points find verification generates a cross, since it is transfixed not by a single line of projection (as in the previous show), but by two, which form four equal angles.

The four points are now, as it were, at the extremities of two intersecting mirrors. Each point is projected sideways onto the mirror surface, instead of striking it directly.

There is no point in leaving the mirror exposed to view in this show, for, in any case, a single surface would not be sufficient.

Furthermore, this symmetry or parity would prevent us from verifying our double optically, shifting the individual's gaze towards the two lateral points which represent the width of the mirror before us, while our reflected image would take shape at the opposite end of another mirror. We see this mirror sideways on, as a knife's edge: indeed it has our own thickness, exactly as it has the thickness of a point.

Optically, therefore, we would be able to perceive only two dimensions. But after the experience of the third, we can imagine the fourth.

The shift from one point to another, between the extremities of the cross, creates a square whose sides become longer or shorter depending on the speed at which we leave one point and approach another.

At minimum speed we have maximum space; and with maximum speed we reach the four points which stick firmly to the central one (still hiding it). For this reason show number four cannot but be 'Time' – the time we take (or which our instruments take) to move from one point to another point within 'The Rooms'. In the exhibition, the terms of time itself are pushed to extremes, beyond the imagination-less dynamic which lines the environment. But here imagination presents itself at the same time as its explanation.

I have loaded the future with memory; and this memory seeps away automatically with every moment that enters the past; while the instruments which mark the passage of time mechanically do not move beyond their mechanism.

29 GENNAIO 1976

 20 MAGGIO 1976

 15 SETTEMBRE 1976

THE ROOMS, FIFTH EXHIBITION

The four months of exhibition which have already passed are the part of the voyage in time which I have covered till now traveling aboard the vehicle 'The Rooms' since October of last year.

As with a missile flashing through the interstellar void, each exhibition materializes as a separate stage which gives way subsequently to another stage, then to a third, and so on.

Thus my research work continues also within the mechanisms which make thought proceed. Indeed, each of these writings on the exhibitions precedes the actual concrete realization of the exhibition to which it refers and follows the moment in which the exhibition has been conceived.

Each separate piece of writing becomes a functional part of the work itself, since its words adjust the trajectory of the imagination while each of the exhibitions adjusts the trajectory of the writing.

Speaking of the previous exhibition, I mentioned the image of a cross consisting of the diagonals of a square indicating a space whose dimensions can be perceived in relation to the dynamic of time. I linked the fourth exhibition to the fourth dimension, but did not describe the work, for it was an experience of the imagination, explained through the turning inside-out of the memory, I did not want the spectator's imagination to come into play outside the place and context which I had decided on for the operation. Why do I say this? Because I want the reader to realize that for me the written work is no more than a part of the engine, which cannot be replaced by another kind of gear.

In the fifth exhibition it is singularity and centrality which are the protagonists. The dimensions vary along with the expansion or contraction of the volumes from or towards that centre on which all diagonals converge. Thus, just as a cube may be any size you like but will always have the same centre, so the rooms now contract and expand physically around their central point.

The work is thus carried out: the three rooms are contained in the middle room, the three rooms are again contained in the middle room of these smaller rooms.

The spectator, proceeding in his visit, re-enters in the rooms three times growing in dimension in relation to them.

THE ROOMS, THE SIXTH EXHIBITION

The sixth exhibition of 'THE ROOMS' might be called the 'Gemelle' (the Twin Girls).

It is seen from the point of view of the father, who produces in his children the widening of his own expressive range. And indeed, 'The Twins' is a doubling of the number three of 'Father, Son and Creativity'.

But the real title of this sixth exhibition ought to be 'L'allontanamento' ('Moving Away'). The father moves away from the children as much as they move away from him. The farewell is the symbol of this parting.

The father, as he moves away, sees the image of his children growing smaller until in the end it disappears entirely. But of course, the children do not get smaller in any real sense, nor do they disappear: they simply retain their own natural dimension, but elsewhere.

A cell divides itself into two eyes which look at each other. They move away from the central point which formerly united them. The facing eye, as it moves away, is transformed from object to image, and begins to grow smaller to leave room for the entire universe of images. While one eye remains on this side, the other on the other side, projects the universe towards it. These two eyes are now here: one at the entrance and one at the far end of the three rooms. Number two is the parity which doubles the disparity of the three rooms making them six. The second exhibition turned reality virtual while making virtuality real. Now, in exhibition number six, the doubling of the rooms is achieved by dividing the two phenomena, the real and the virtual, as if they two were entering the mechanism of our optical perspective. Thus in this case the reproduction gives up the actual, total replacement of the gallery, as real space welcomes the reproduction.

In this operation the twins which greet one, from the far end of the gallery, are brought into the foreground in the scale which the photographic eye has registered from a distance. Through this scale we see the twins reproduced natural size at the far end of the 'real' gallery. Thus our seeing eye will now reduce their dimension to the same scale as the photographic foreground.

The dimensions of the two opposite poles are maintained constant by perspective as it runs back and forth between the rooms.

NUMBER SEVEN OF 'THE ROOMS'

This is the second time we encounter the number seven.

We found it in the first exhibition, when it was used to identify one-ness, singularity, the un-doubled. In the story of the rooms, number six is the half-way mark. The number seven means that I am now writing the first of the other six pages which, ideally, will come to rest on the first six so as to bring to a close my text of 'The Rooms'.

What, then, is the difference between the seventh exhibition and the first?

The seventh is, as it were, the mirror of the first. In the first a mirror was set so as to 'imitate' the six openings or doorways (three real and three reflected); whereas in the seventh the six openings (real and reflected) imitate the mirror.

And I – between these two reflecting exhibitions – recognize myself as the creative point.

I shall create this exhibition by breaking a corner of the mirror, placed once again at the far end of the rooms. I shall apply some plaster to the inside of the doorways so as to give the openings the same new shape as the mirror. Thus these openings will be 'false' – both on this side and the other side of the mirror – while the mirror itself will be its real shape.

NUMBER EIGHT OF 'THE ROOMS'

I would not trouble, in the case of this eighth exhibition, to point out its over-turning on the previous exhibitions, except to indicate its direction in the development of the signs of parity.

In this exhibition, positive and negative, like fullness and emptiness, are inter-twined without allowing us to make out the point of interchange between reality and image which I identify with the mirror.

Thus, mingling the imagined vision with the physical one, the eye may set out either from the entrance or from the far wall beyond the three openings, passing either through the 'fullness' of the wall or through the empty space.

The image I present here is that of fullness corresponding to the dimensions of the first opening, but seen in perspective, standing at the other end of the room. The perspective of fullness is introduced into the perspective of empty space which I see from this side of the rooms.

The sum resulting from the count-up of the full and empty spaces is number eight.

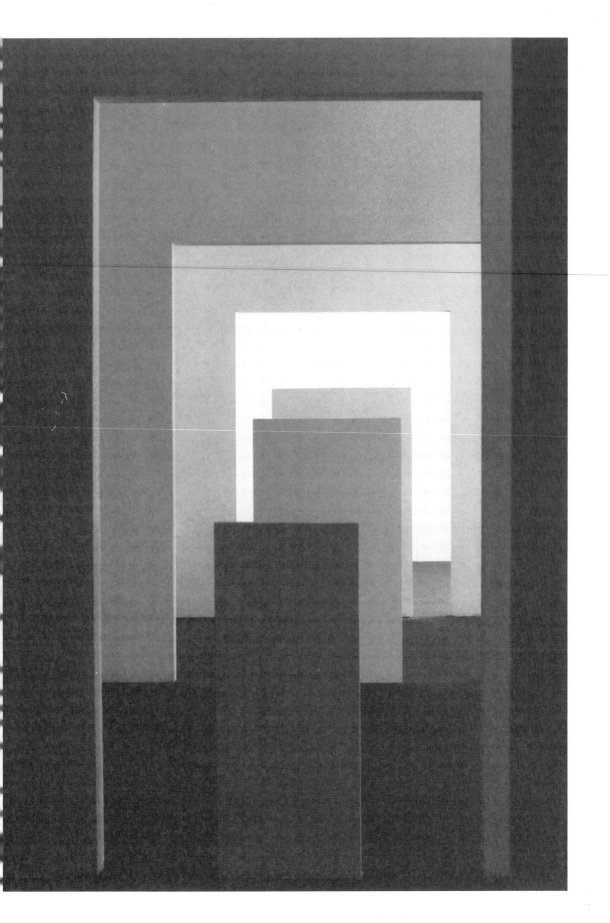

'THE ROOMS: NINE'

I have never been to my mother's grave.

It would seem to me a rather odd thing to do.

Dante uses the number nine to indicate the perfect rings, which, in the 'Divine Comedy', represent his wandering through the 'Inferno'.

My ninth exhibition in 'The Rooms' is the visit to hell. But its title is 'L'avvicinamento' ('Approach').

In number six, the daughters moved away from the father, whereas here it is the mother who comes closer to the son.

Dante does not visit the 'Inferno' by actually entering it, but by bringing its symbols on the pages of his work. Thus my own visit will stop at the first of the three openings of 'The Rooms', while the stone which seals off the world in which my mother now lives will be placed against the far wall of the gallery. This stone will appear as a virtual threshold, separating two forms of a single reality.

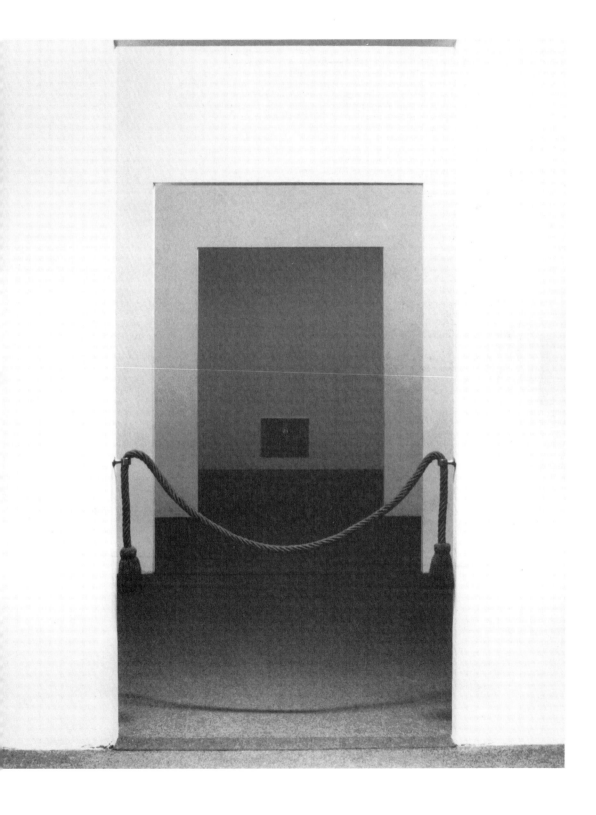

THE TENTH MOMENT IS THAT OF THE REAL ROOMS

GALLERIA CHRISTIAN STEIN
Piazza S. Carlo 206, III p.
IOI2I TORINO
Tel. OII/53.55.74

                                        Venezia, 7 luglio I976

            IL DECIMO MOMENTO E' QUELLO DELLE STANZE REALI

                                   Michelangelo Pistoletto

dal 20 luglio al 20 agosto

orario della galleria:
tutti i giorni dalle I5,30 alle 20
nelle altre ore per appuntamento
lunedì chiuso.

THE ROOMS: CHAPTER ELEVEN

During my first night in Venice this year, I dreamed of a sequence of Baroque rooms. While dreaming, in a brief moment of lucid awareness, I studied the images carefully, and noticed that the rooms were all perfect in every detail of style, totally consistent, without the slightest degree of uncertainty or interruption; yet it wouldn't have been an easy task to describe or draw them with anything like the same degree of precision. Thus I realized that even the most ignorant of men can dream 'in perfect style' like a camera. But after my dream I had occasion to visit a number of Venetian houses, with Baroque rooms in which I found the same perfection of image. Here, too, no part of any wall was without its stylistically perfect detail.

These real rooms are the physical exposition of the single dream of the person who imagined them.

The title of this eleventh chapter is 'Il transferimento' (The transfer).

What had happened was that in coming to Venice my 'rooms' had become overlaid with Baroque dreams which I now translate into physical terms, transferring their image onto the pages of this review (1).

The white rectangle interrupts the eleventh image as a break in the dream.

The white walls of 'The Rooms' in Turin are the ideal support for the reality of the paper:.

(1) 'Le Citta di Riga', Edizioni La Nuova Foglio, Pollenza (Macerata)

IN SEPTEMBER 1976 THE STEIN GALLERY IN TURIN SENT A PAGE PRINTED COMPLETELY IN BLACK AND WITHOUT ANY TEXT TO ALL THOSE WHO HAD RECEIVED THE PRECEDING 11 PAGES OF INFORMATION. THIS PAGE WAS SIMULTANEOUSLY AN ANNOUNCEMENT AND REALIZATION OF THE TWELFTH EXHIBITION.

Site

The site is a place where a piece should be but isn't.

(Smithson in Bear and Sharp 1996: 249–50)

Where minimalism's site-specificity is held *within* the gallery, the approaches to specific sites which emerged in its wake around land art, earth art, and conceptual art frequently played on the gallery as a vantage point from which the viewer might look *out* toward designated, mapped locations. Typically incorporating a mapping or documentation of places and events, these practices reflected upon and revised the impulse of earlier environmental art, happening performance, and Fluxus presentations, among others, to test the limits and discourses of the work of art by directing attention toward conventionally 'non-art' occurrences, locations, and acts. Here, the early work of Robert Smithson, Dennis Oppenheim, and Douglas Huebler, in particular, treated the gallery as a place to document or map interventions into inaccessible sites, a gesture which, Oppenheim argues, countered 'major canons of traditional art' through the fact that 'you can't see the art, you can't buy the art, you can't have the art' (Kaye 1996: 66). Reading the site in terms of its *absences*, and so focusing upon the elusiveness of the actual or 'real' site, this work articulated its specificity to site through means quite different from minimalism's engagement with 'the present tense of space' (Morris 1993c). In doing so, these strategies clarify relationships between the work and its site operating through a wide range of site-specific practices.

Mapping Site: Robert Smithson

Created in the year that the *Earthworks* exhibition at the Dwan Gallery, New York, first brought attention to land art or earth art as a genre of work, the late Robert Smithson's series of Non-Sites of 1968 present materials which have been collected from designated outdoor sites, deposited in bins whose construction echoes a simple, clean, minimalist aesthetic, and set in the gallery beside information tracing out the geographical or geological characteristics of the area from which they have been removed. Rather than evoke the properties of the particular place they evidence, however, the Non-Site's juxtaposition of 'undifferentiated' material and 'mapped' information reveals Smithson's incapacity, or reluctance, to simulate this location in the gallery. As the term itself suggests, the Non-Site asserts, first of all, that the site against which it claims definition is elsewhere. In the face of these 'large, abstract maps made into three dimensions' (Flam 1996: 181), Smithson argues, '[w]hat you are really confronted with [. . .] is the absence of the site [. . .] a very ponderous, weighty absence' (Lippard and Smithson 1996: 193).

Characterising his encounter with the 'specific site[s]' (Smithson 1996: 60) which he had been visiting and subsequently mapping since 1965 in terms of a 'suspension of *boundaries*' (Smithson 1996a: 103), 'a "de-architecturing"' which 'takes place before the artist sets his limits' (Smithson 1996a: 104), Smithson describes his interest in looking beyond the white walls of the gallery in terms of a resistance to the closure of the conventional art object. 'Most of the better artists,' he writes, 'prefer processes that have not been idealised, or differentiated into "objective" meanings' (Smithson 1996a: 101). Setting his experience of these sites against the sculptor Tony Smith's celebrated 1966 account of his drive across the partly constructed New Jersey Turnpike, where the 'road and much of the landscape was artificial, and yet it couldn't be called a work of art', Smithson argues that Smith

is talking about a sensation, not a finished work of art [he] is
describing the state of his mind in the 'primary process' of
making contact with matter. This process is called by Anton
Ehrenzweig 'dedifferentiation,' and it involves a suspended
question regarding 'limitlessness'.

(Smithson 1996a: 102–3)

Rather than describe the site as a given topology or geography,
Smithson recalls a particular kind of encounter, a certain perceptual
exposure. Thus, he proposes, in returning from the site, '[t]he artist
who is physically engulfed tries to give evidence of this experience
through a limited (mapped) revision of the original unbounded state'
(Smithson 1996a: 104).

In this context, it is in its function as a map, in its very attempt to
present or point to the site, that the Non-Site asserts its antithetical
relationship to these 'outdoor collections of undifferentiated material'
(Smithson and Wheeler 1996: 221). Indeed, in its designation of a location's specific properties, its limits and boundaries, the Non-Site effects
precisely the kind of imposition in whose suspension Smithson supposes
the site is experienced. Even in so far as the Non-Site casts the very
idea of a work over a specific site, then it threatens to efface precisely
that unbounded state Smithson seeks to map. Here, in fact, the Non-
Site reproduces the gallery's contradictory attempt to recollect, and so
limit, the 'dedifferentiated' site. Thus, where the experience of site is
one of a limitlessness, the Non-Site establishes itself as a limiting mechanism, a differentiation, whose effect is not so much to expose the site
as to erase it. Smithson observes that '[t]he site has no seeming limits,
but the Non-Site points to the site. In a sense the Non-Site, although
it points to it, effaces this particular region' (Smithson and Wheeler
1996: 198).

As this suggests, however, Smithson's Non-Site points to the site,
first of all, by exposing the limits and operation of the gallery itself.
Indeed, Smithson polarises the relationship between Non-Site and site
around the art object and the gallery's differentiating function. Stating

that '[a]ll legitimate art deals with limits' (Lippard and Smithson 1996: 194), Smithson repeatedly emphasises in his published writing and interviews that 'the [Non-Site] really comes out of a comprehension of limits' (Smithson and Toner: 234), stressing the abstract nature of its 'limited (mapped) revision' and subsequent removal from the site. Whereas the experience of site is of material *scattered*, Smithson notes, the 'bins or containers of my Non-Sites gather *in* the fragments' (Smithson 1996a: 104), mirroring the gallery's confinement, and effecting a 'containment within the containment of the room' (Smithson and Wheeler 1996: 204). The Non-Site, in fact, reproduces and works over the limits of the gallery, exposing the *absence* of the site in an exacerbation of the gallery's objectifying function.

In this respect, the Non-Site foregrounds its indexical function as a map, its mechanisms of referral, and deferral, over and above any claim to present the properties of a place. In his contribution to the definitive catalogue of Smithson's sculpture (Hobbs 1981), the critic Lawrence Alloway argues that the relation of Non-Site to site is 'like that of language to the world: it is a signifier and the Site is that which is signified. It is not the referent but the language system which is in the foreground' (Alloway 1981: 42). As signifier, however, the Non-Site functions in the absence of a stable signified. Indeed, in foregrounding the inability of the object or the gallery to present the site, the Non-Site reveals this *absence* as the condition of its own mapping.

In his own account of the origins and development of the Non-Site, Smithson emphasises precisely the link with his 'concerns for mapping' (Smithson and Wheeler 1996: 212). As its antithesis, Smithson suggests, the Non-Site prompts a dialectical reading of the site. Speaking at a Symposium at Cornell University in early 1969, Smithson recounted his development of 'a dialectic that involved what I call site and non-site' in which 'I would set limits in terms of this dialogue (it's a back and forth rhythm that goes between indoors and outdoors)' (Flam 1996: 178). Indeed, this prompt not only emphasises the Non-Sites' functioning as an index to the site, but in the site's absence, serves to trace out the contradictions of mapping itself. In a footnote to his essay 'The Spiral Jetty' of 1972, Smithson tabulated this relationship:

Dialectic of Site and Non-Site

Site		*Non-Site*
1.	Open limits	Closed limits
2.	A Series of Points	An Array of Matter
3.	Outer Coordinates	Inner Coordinates
4.	Subtraction	Addition
5.	Indeterminate (Certainty)	Determinate (Uncertainty)
6.	Scattered (Information)	Contained (Information)
7.	Reflection	Mirror
8.	Edge	Centre
9.	Some Place (physical)	No Place (abstract)
10.	Many	One

(Smithson 1996b: 152–3)

As antithesis, Smithson argues, the closed limits of the Non-Site's singular, centred, material focus can, in fact, 'only be approached in terms of its own negation' (Lippard and Smithson 1996: 193). In this sense, the Non-Site points back toward the site as its point of origin. Yet it is also in this antithetical relationship to the site that the limits of the Non-Site are set.

If, as a material, quantifiable focus, the Non-Site must 'be approached in terms of its own negation', then its very antithetical definition of the site, as absent, immaterial, and unavailable, forces a continual return to the Non-Site. Characterising the Non-Sites as prompting 'mental disasters, convergences that couldn't converge, and polarities that never quite met' (Smithson and Wheeler 1996: 212), Smithson clearly understood this dialectical relationship to imply a convergence which is out of reach. The relationship of Non-Site to site, here, is not one of a simple or stable *opposition*, but dialectical *movement*. Qualifying the 'Dialectic of Site and Non-Site', he remarks that:

The range of convergence between Site and Non-Site consists of a course of hazards, a double path made up of signs, photographs and maps that belong to both sides of the dialectic at once. Both sides are present and absent at the same time [. . .] Two-dimensional and three-dimensional things trade places with each other in the range of convergence. Large scale becomes small. Small scale becomes large. A point on a map expands to the size of the land mass. A land mass contracts to a point.

(Smithson 1996b: 153)

The site, it follows, is not available as an 'object', for it is not static: the site is mobile, always in a process of appearance or disappearance, available only in a dialectical move which the Non-Site prompts and to which it always returns. The site, in fact, is an effect of mapping, yet always remains antithetical to the map. The Non-Site, then, prompts a dialectical move toward the site which cannot be resolved, and so a movement which calls into question the status and solidity of both Non-Site and site. It is a 'dialectic of place' (Flam 1996: 187), Smithson observes, which 'just goes on permuting itself into this endless doubling, so that you have the nonsite functioning as a mirror and the site functioning as a reflection. Existence becomes a doubtful thing' (Lippard and Smithson 1996: 193).

For the architect Peter Eisenman, in his questioning of 'traditional geometries and processes in architecture' (Eisenman 1986: 4), site is precisely a function of absence. Observing that 'absence is either the trace of a previous presence, it contains *memory*; or the trace of a possible presence, it contains *immanence*' (Eisenman 1986: 4–5), Eisenman reads site as complex and multiple, always subject to absence's processes of disappearance and appearance. Whereas in architecture '[a] presence is a physically real form, whether a solid, such as a building, or a void, such as a space between two buildings' (Eisenman 1986: 4–5), site 'can be thought of as non-static' (Eisenman 1986: 5–6). Thus, Eisenman emphasises, 'To privilege "the site" as *the* context is to repress the other possible con*texts*, is to become fixated on the presences of

"the site," is to believe that "the site" exists as a permanent knowable whole. Such a belief [he concludes] is untenable today' (Eisenman
1986: 5).

The Non-Site, in fact, marks this unavailability of site as 'presence'
or 'object', prompting a rhythm of appearance and disappearance which
challenges the concept of the site as a permanent knowable whole. Here
the site is neither that which *it was*, a stable point of origin, nor that
which *will be*, a specific, 'knowable' point of destination.

This mobility of the site, its capacity to elude resolution into a static
object, is discovered even in the most literal address to the Non-Site as
an index of the site. Smithson's selection of specific sites, their geography
and physical characteristics, underwrites the effect of the Non-Site.
Smithson's selection of sites seems to be linked to an attitude or frame
of mind. In the determination of a particular site, he suggests, '[t]here
is no wilful choice. A site at zero degree, where the material strikes the
mind, where absences become apparent, appeals to me' (Lippard and
Smithson 1996: 194).

Smithson's attitude echoes that described by Marcel Duchamp in his
selection of 'Readymades', banal, largely unaltered, functional objects
chosen by Duchamp, usually signed, and placed in the gallery as challenges to the conceptual frameworks defining the art object. Speaking
'Apropos of Ready-mades' in New York in 1961, at the time of his
resurgent influence on art and performance, Duchamp argued that in
the selection of such objects as *Bottle Dryer* (1914), a snow shovel under
the title *In Advance of the Broken Arm* (1914) and an upturned urinal as
Fountain (1917), his choice 'was never dictated by aesthetic delectation.
This choice was based on a reaction of visual indifference with at the
same time a total absence of good or bad taste [. . .] in fact a complete
anaesthesia' (Sanouillet and Peterson 1975: 141). Smithson's account of
his reasons for choosing specific sites strikes a similar chord, reflecting
a sense of geographic and mental drift and aesthetic ambivalence. In
determining which sites to map, he notes:

There is no hope for logic. If you try to come up with a logical
reason then you might as well forget it, because it doesn't deal
with any kind of nameable, measurable situation. All dimension
seems to be lost in the process. In other words, you are really
going from some place to some place, which is to say, nowhere in
particular [. . .] There's a suspension of destination.

(Lippard and Smithson 1996: 194)

Indeed, despite his note on *A Nonsite, Franklin, New Jersey* (1968), and
other such pieces, that 'Tours to sites are possible', these sites do not
offer an effective point of destination in which to resolve the Non-Site's
deferral of attention. The Non-Site, Smithson emphasises, 'is a map
that will take you somewhere, but when you get there you won't really
know where you are' (Bear and Sharp 1996: 249). For Smithson, clearly,
his experience at these geographical sites is no less a sense of the absence
of the site than that which confronts the viewer in the gallery. Thus,
he suggests, while the Non-Site directs the viewer toward specific
'points of collection', these 'tend to be scattered throughout the site'
such that

once you get there, there's no destination. Or if there is
information, the information is so low level it doesn't focus on
any particular spot . . . so the site is evading you all the while it's
directing you to it [. . .] There is no object to go toward. In the
very name 'Non-Site' you're really making a reference to a
particular site but that particular site evades itself, or it's
incognito [. . .] The location is held in suspense.

(Smithson and Wheeler 1996: 218)

Here, there is no authentic, original site to be grasped as that to
which the Non-Site refers, or any 'permanent knowable whole' which
can transcend its mapping function. Indeed, paradoxically, where the
'limited (mapped) revision' in the gallery threatens to efface the site,
the site cannot be read, represented, or thought without mapping.

In the absence of the map, then, the site is in suspension, incognito. In fact, as its reflection, the site cannot even be seen without the Non-Site. It is in this context that the Non-Site traces out a more complex mapping, one that embraces the site's absences. Noting that '[m]aps are very elusive things' (Bear and Sharp 1996: 249), Smithson's emphasis upon the dialectical move prompted by the Non-Site echoes Edward Soja's more recent analysis of *Postmodern Geographies* (Soja 1989) in which he stresses the map's definition of 'a geography of simultaneous relations and meanings' (Soja 1989: 1), a simultaneity which language tends to betray. He continues:

> What one sees when one looks at geographies is stubbornly simultaneous, but language dictates a sequential succession, a linear flow of sentential statements bound by the most spatial of earthly constraints, the impossibility of two objects (words) occupying the same precise place (as on a page).
>
> (Soja 1989: 2)

The Non-Site's 'mapping' emerges, finally, in the *restlessness* of this relationship; in the *possibility* of the Non-Site's convergence with the 'Site', in the *implication* of one in the other, and so in the 'bipolar rhythm between mind and matter' (Flam 1996: 187) it produces. Here, 'the site is a place where the work should be but isn't' (Bear and Sharp 1996: 249–50): the site appears in *the promise* of its occupation by the Non-Site, where a recognition of the site assumes the absence of the work, yet the work is a necessary index to the site. Indeed, the Non-Site's site-specificity is an effect of this contradiction, in which the work and the site threaten to occupy, and be defined in, the same precise place.

Unmappable Spaces

In working to expose the absence of the map's original, authentic referent, Smithson's Non-Sites engage with the paradoxes of mapping essentially unmappable spaces. Indeed, in this respect, the Non-Site reproduces the effect de Certeau ascribes to the 'symbolic (named)' (de Certeau 1984: 103), where representation *moves one on* from the site. It is in this context that the Non-Site's mapping is realised as always in process, always contingent, temporary, where the representation of site is always subject to being written over. Here, too, the Non-Site suggests a mapping which can be linked to various readings of the peculiarities of contemporary place and space, and which is symptomatic of approaches to site in performance.

In his major study of *Postmodernism, or, The Cultural Logic of Late Capitalism* (Jameson 1991), Frederic Jameson identifies conceptual art with tactics closely aligned to those of Smithson's Non-Sites. Here, Jameson suggests, 'on the occasion of what first seems to be an encounter with a work of art of some kind, the categories of the mind itself – normally not conscious [. . .] are flexed, their structuring presence now felt laterally by the viewer like musculature or nerves of which we normally remain insensible' (Jameson 1991: 157). Emphasising '[t]he relationship between the vocation of such conceptual art and some of the classic texts of deconstruction' (Jameson 1991: 157), Jameson goes on to propose that certain manifestations of this 'dissolution of inherited form' (Jameson 1991: 157) may be extended toward a 'cognitive mapping' (Jameson 1991: 416) of contemporary spatial, social, or institutional relations and effects.

In defining cognitive mapping, Jameson draws on his reading of Kevin Lynch's celebrated study of *The Image of the City* (Lynch 1960). Proposing, Jameson tells us, that 'urban alienation is directly proportional to the mental unmappability of local cityscapes' (Jameson 1991: 415), Lynch's study addresses the individual's sense of disparity between the 'here and now of immediate perception and the imaginative or imaginary sense of the city as an absent totality' (Jameson 1991: 411).

In the context of de Certeau's later account of the realisation of place in spatial practices, Lynch's study can be understood as addressing the individual's capacity to resolve their own practice of the city into the order they imagine it implies. In this way, Jameson reports, in inviting his subjects 'to draw their city context from memory' in order that he might distinguish the differing effects of contrasting urban designs, Lynch concludes that

> A city like Boston [. . .] with its monumental perspective, its
> markers and statuary, its combination of grand but simple spatial
> forms, including dramatic boundaries such as the Charles River,
> not only allows people to have, in their imaginations, a generally
> successful and continuous location to the rest of the city, but
> gives them something of the freedom and aesthetic gratification
> of [a] traditional city.
>
> (Jameson 1991: 415)

In his approach to post-modernism, Jameson extends this address to a disparity between individual experience and an imagined 'absent totality'. Where Lynch engages with a phenomenology of the city, however, Jameson extends his analysis toward ideology's attempt to 'span or co-ordinate, to map' the gap between the 'local positioning of the individual subject' and an 'imaginary totality' (Jameson 1991: 416) characterised, in the post-modern, by a resistance to unified, clear and stable positions or systems of belief.

For Jameson, 'post-modernist' art and architecture are symptomatic of this contemporary dilemma, in which the resolution of the individual's practice into a 'known' spatial, social, or ideological totality has come under question. In this context, Jameson cites John Portman's Westin Bonaventure Hotel in the new Los Angeles downtown area as producing a specifically 'post-modernist space' (Jameson 1991: 45) where the individual's sense of location is radically undermined. Reading the Bonaventure as 'aspiring to being a total space, a complete world, a kind of miniature city' (Jameson 1991: 40), Jameson emphasises the discontinuities in which these architectural spaces take their effect. First of all, he proposes, the building asserts a strongly discontinuous relationship to its city surroundings. The Bonaventure's reflective glass skin 'repels the city outside, a repulsion for which we have analogies in those reflector sunglasses which make it impossible for your interlocutor to see your own eyes' so achieving 'a peculiar and placeless dissociation' (Jameson 1991: 42). Where from the outside the building achieves 'a certain aggressivity toward and power over the Other' such that 'you cannot see the hotel itself but only the distorted images of everything that surrounds it' (Jameson 1991: 42), its internal architecture amplifies this difficulty of establishing one's *place*. On entering the building, Jameson notes, the pedestrian must negotiate the unpredictable relationships between the hotel's external structure and its internal spaces. In these spaces, the pedestrian becomes subject to 'a new collective practice, a new mode in which individuals move and congregate, something like the practice of a new and historically original kind of hypercrowd' (Jameson 1991: 40). In fact, Portman's building is defined not simply in the pedestrian's movement through it, but *in movement itself*, as if the architecture had usurped the visitor's capacity to negotiate its spaces. Here, Jameson tells us, 'escalators and elevators [. . .] replace movement but also, and above all, designate themselves as new reflexive signs and emblems of movement proper' such that 'the narrative stroll has been underscored, symbolized, reified, and replaced by a transportation machine' (Jameson 1991: 42). Amid this building's spatial discontinuities and appropriation and simulation of movement, the visitor cannot easily put these architectural spaces in their place. Instead, Jameson concludes, the visitor is confronted by 'a constant busyness' that 'gives the feeling that emptiness here is absolutely packed, that it is an element within which you yourself are immersed, without any of that distance that formerly enabled the perception of perspective or volume. You are in this hyperspace up to your eyes and your body' (Jameson 1991: 43).

For the pedestrian, this building works against the perspective and order mapping would install, exposing the gap between the visitor's immediate spatial practice and their sense of an implied totality. Indeed, Jameson concludes that the Bonaventure offers a terrain in which it is simply 'quite impossible to get your bearings'. Recently, he continues, 'colour coding and directional signs have been added in a pitiful and revealing, rather desperate, attempt to restore the co-ordinates of an older space' (Jameson 1991: 44).

In opening this rift between immediate spatial experience and its location, this 'new post-modernist space' (Jameson 1991: 44) forces a continual rereading or rewriting of the order implied in spatial practice. Indeed, here, the visitor's effort to locate their practice is continually subject to a rewriting. In this context, cognitive mapping, a term, Jameson tells us, 'which was meant to have a kind of oxymoronic value and to transcend the limits of mapping altogether' (Jameson 1991: 416), characterises an address to precisely this gap, or disparity, this movement between practice and place. Here, Jameson considers a mapping which is constantly *in motion*, and which reflects the nature of post-modernist space. 'In this new machine,' he remarks, 'which does not, like the older modernist machinery of the locomotive or the aeroplane, represent motion, but which can only be represented *in motion*, something of the mystery of the new post-modernist space concentrated' (Jameson 1991: 45). Where post-modernist space exposes the inability of spatial practice to rest in the order it implies, so a cognitive mapping of the Bonaventure might direct attention toward an architectural terrain, or totality, which evades the co-ordinates mapping imposes upon it. Here, in fact, cognitive mapping functions in this very sense of *lacking a place*, as if tracing the co-ordinates of a terrain from which it is continually displaced.

This sense of a terrain which evades the co-ordinates of the map is also evident in site-specific work rehearsing a transitive definition of site. Here, where the site-specific work foregrounds site's elusiveness and mobility, the concept and features of the site which it articulates are continually annulled, displaced, or surpassed. In this context, one might read Forced Entertainment's exposure of the effect of the 'symbolic (named)', or Brith Gof's articulation of an incongruent and 'deeply fractured' (McLucas, Morgan and Pearson 1995: 51) relationship between 'host' (the site) and 'ghost' (the work), as exposing the site's evasion of the specific co-ordinates in which the site-specific work would establish its location.

In Smithson's own work this sense of dislocation extends to the literal co-ordinates of a mapped place. In analysing Smithson's most celebrated work, *Spiral Jetty* (1970), in *Earthwards: Robert Smithson and Art After Babel* (Shapiro 1995), Gary Shapiro stresses not only the literal difficulty of approaching the Jetty, which, at an obscure point on the Great Salt Lake in Utah, projects 1,500 feet into its waters, but the difficulty of locating *Spiral Jetty* as a work at all. Arguing that 'the multiple referents of the title *Spiral Jetty*' suggest 'that there is no primary, authentic object' to which other expressions of the piece are 'ancillary' (Shapiro 1995: 7), Shapiro reads the piece across Smithson's arrangement of rocks in the Great Salt Lake, a film that recounts its making, and an essay in which Smithson 'discusses the spiral and the film in language ranging through mythopoetic, art historical and geological modes' (Shapiro 1995: 7). In doing so, Shapiro argues that this work is constituted as a series of texts, each of which implies but is displaced from a centre, and which have themselves then been reproduced and dispersed again (Shapiro 1995: 8–9). For Shapiro, this textual dispersal is reflected upon in the film, where Smithson's voice-over reveals the 'senselessness of the Jetty's centre', intoning:

> From the centre of the Spiral Jetty
> North – Mud, salt crystals, rocks, water
> North by East – Mud, salt crystals,
>   rocks, water
> Northeast by North – Mud, salt crystals,
>   rocks, water
> Northeast by East – Mud, salt crystals,
>   rocks, water

(Shapiro 1995: 16–17)

Far from making the *Spiral Jetty* available, Smithson's co-ordinates mimic the indexical function of a map but fail to locate, or state, its place. Instead, the *Spiral Jetty* is located in the inter-leaving and over-laying of texts, and so in a continual deferral from one point to another. Here, *Spiral Jetty*, as Shapiro suggests, exists, and is mapped, concep-tually, in this process of deferral, in the gaps and disparities between texts and locations, where the real work and its real site evade the specific, mapped co-ordinates it presents. Here, in fact, Smithson's work indicates again something of the paradoxical nature of these approaches to site, where site-specific practice works against its own final or defin-itive location precisely in order to expose the unstable, evasive, and shifting nature of this place.

Performing Mapping: Allan Kaprow, Claes Oldenburg, Wolf Vostell

This functioning of the site-specific work is reflected in early entries into 'environmental' performance. For Allan Kaprow and Claes Oldenburg, working in New York in the late 1950s and early 1960s, as well as the German artist Wolf Vostell, the approach to 'site' through performance closely linked phenomenological enquiries into art-viewing with a testing of the morphology and limits of the artwork. Here, performance provided a means through which the geography and events of 'found' sites could be approached outside the representational terms of painting and sculpture. Indeed, in approaching 'real' places (Oldenburg 1965: 200), Kaprow's happenings 'for performers only', Oldenburg's 'happenings of place' (Oldenburg 1973), and Vostell's 'dé-coll/age happenings' reflected on relationships between practice and place, and so work and site, fostering unpredictable, fluid exchanges between the frame of an artwork and its various contexts.

This address to the limits of the artwork emerged in the context of inter-disciplinary challenges to the conventional enclosure of the object and a resultant series of moves from conventional visual art practices into performance. For the Fluxus artist Dick Higgins, identifying 'hybrid' forms between music and philosophy (John Cage), music and sculpture (Joe Jones), and poetry and sculpture (Robert Fillou) (Higgins 1969: 27), the 'intermedial' art practices of the early 1960s challenged the viewer's ability to resolve and stabilise identities and so effectively map the co-ordinates of a work. Reflecting on the early development of performance by artists, Higgins identified the difficulty of formally locating an object or practice as a key aspect of its effect, observing that '[t]he Happening developed as an intermedium, an uncharted land that lies between collage, music and theatre [. . .] The concept itself is best defined in terms of what it is not, rather than by what it is' (Higgins 1969: 25).

John Cage's untitled event at Black Mountain College of the Summer of 1952, which acted as a key precursor and influence on Happening performance, was defined in precisely such a challenge to the integrity of conventional forms. Organised around 'an empty centre' (Cage and Charles 1981: 165), this event brought Cage's own compositional methods to bear on the notion of a 'multi-dimensional theatre' (Cage and Charles 1981: 166) defined by the French visionary and poet Antonin Artaud. In an interview published in 1981, Cage recounted that 'we decided to divide the audience into four triangles whose peaks would be directed toward an empty centre. [. . .] the action wasn't supposed to occur in the centre, but everywhere around the audience. That is, in the four corners, in the gaps, and also from above' (Cage and Charles 1981: 165).

Following Merce Cunningham's interest 'in the problems of assembling heterogeneous facts' (Cage and Charles 1981: 164), Cage had sought to effect a 'co-existence of dissimilars' (Cage 1968: 12) and so create a situation in which conflicting aesthetic logics would be simultaneously in play and where none of the works constituting the event would be free from the noise, or interruptions, of others. As Cage read a forty-five minute lecture, poems by M.C. Richards and Charles Olsen, performed, like Cage's text, from various ladders positioned around the room, were set alongside 'piano by David Tudor' and 'films projected on the walls' (Cage and Charles 1981: 165). Robert Rauschenberg's white canvases of 1952 could be seen hung from the ceiling. Rauschenberg himself 'played old records on an antique phonograph' (Cage 1981: 165). While these events unfolded and overlapped, the choreographer and dancer Merce Cunningham improvised freely around performers and spectators. Rather than establish 'a *finite temporal object* with a beginning, middle and an end' (Cage and Charles 1981: 51), Cage understood this overlaying of works to prompt the viewer's simultaneous perception of distinct and different spaces and perspectives. In such a situation, he argues, 'space arises out of the fact that the works are super-imposed and accumulate their own spaces. There is no single space, finally – there are several spaces and these spaces tend to multiply among themselves' (Cage and Charles 1981: 132).

Allan Kaprow's entry into performance from 1958 extended this address to disparate and discontinuous events and spaces. Indeed, in these contexts Kaprow's early performance looked toward the incursion of 'real space' and so 'real time' into the viewer's experience, in a breaking down of the frame of a work in favour of engagements with 'everyday' places and events. Here, though, Kaprow not only drew on Cage's concepts and procedures but also contemporary readings of Jackson Pollock's celebrated 'drip' or 'action' paintings and their implication for the creative process and relationships between 'literal space' and 'painted space' (Kaprow 1993a: 11).

In the mid-1950s, Pollock's 'drip' paintings became a focus of a critical valorisation of the artist's engagement in the creative act. For the abstract expressionist painter, the critic Harold Rosenberg famously argued, the canvas had come to offer 'an arena in which to act – rather than a space in which to reproduce, re-design' where '[w]hat was to go onto the canvas was not a picture but an event' (Rosenberg 1959: 40). In this context, Rosenberg concluded, the contemporary vitality of Pollock's paintings lay in their definition of a tension between object and event. Writing in 1958, E.C. Goossen proposed that this tension was amplified by the sheer size of Pollock's paintings. Crediting Pollock and Barnett Newman with the introduction of a new scale in painting, Goossen read Pollock's work as exemplifying the effect of 'the Big Canvas' (Goossen 1973: 61), a canvas he defined as 'in both directions [. . .] larger than the comprehensive image the eye is capable of taking in' (Goossen 1973: 58). Denied the figure or perspective, he concluded, the viewer is left to negotiate this surface in relation to her own presence and definition of a perceptual field and so between its surfaces and the space she occupies. Writing of 'The Legacy of Jackson Pollock' in the same year, Kaprow looked from this tension toward performance, concluding that 'we do not enter a painting of Pollock's in any one place (or hundred places). Anywhere is everywhere [. . .] Pollock ignored the confines of the rectangular field in favour of a continuum going in all directions simultaneously, beyond the literal dimensions of any work' (Kaprow 1993: 5).

Here, Kaprow suggests, where the 'space' of the painting 'is not clearly palpable as such' (Kaprow 1993: 6), the artist might be prompted to move off the canvas, 'to give up the making of paintings entirely' (Kaprow 1993: 7) and so enter into the space before and around the canvas. Where Pollock 'left us at the point where we must become preoccupied with and even dazzled by the space and objects of our everyday life' (Kaprow 1993: 7), Kaprow concludes, a new art should look *outward*, toward imbrications of 'virtual' and 'real' spaces and so toward an 'environmental' art. In his 'Notes on the Creation of a Total Art' of 1958, Kaprow suggests that

> if we join a literal space and a painted space, and these two spaces
> to a sound, we achieve the 'right' relationship by considering
> each component in quantity and quality on an imaginary scale
> [. . .] The 'balance' (if one wants to call it that) is primarily an
> environmental one.
>
> (Kaprow 1993a: 11)

It is in these contexts that Kaprow's Happenings 'for performers only' provide structures through which the viewer-participant acts out a tracing of a work over discontinuous spaces. Indeed, although Kaprow developed performances for built and found environments from 1959, including *18 Happenings in 6 Parts** from which the term happening was coined, it is this form which he adopted from 1964 which fully develops the implications of this entry into an 'environmental' space. In the happenings for performers only, those who would be an audience to the happening are invited to participate in the performance of a set of programmed activities realised in unconventional or 'non-art' contexts and dispersed in space and time. Typically, for *Household* (1964), realised by participants in 'a lonesome dump out in the country' (Kaprow 1966a: 6), *Soap* (1965), played out over two mornings and evenings in public sites chosen by the performers (Kaprow 1966a: 8), and *Calling* (1965), in which activities were dispersed across New York City and subsequently in a farm in New Jersey (Kaprow 1995: 195), would-be participants meet in advance of their 'performance' to discuss the patterns and triggers for activities. Subsequently, Kaprow stresses, '[t]he happening is performed according to plan but without rehearsal, audience, or repetition' (Kaprow 1966a: 3). In this situation 'pre-knowledge of the Happening's cluster of events by all participants will allow each one to make his own connections' (Kaprow 1966: 191). In this way, individuals complete their tasks often in isolation or at one remove from activities occurring elsewhere or in relation to events at another time or actions subject to the choices, inclinations, and circumstances of other performers. In the score for *Soap*, then, where 'actions given in parentheses are alternatives given to the participant' (Kaprow 1966a: 10), Kaprow's plan states:

1ˢᵗ morning:	clothes dirtied by urination
1ˢᵗ evening:	clothes washed
	(in the sea)
	(in the laundromat)

* Kaprow's earliest performance work includes an untitled piece presented at Douglass College, New Brunswick, 15 April 1958, as well as an unperformed script entitled *The Demiurge* dated spring 1959 (Sohm 1970).

2nd morning:	cars dirtied with jam on a busy street
	cars cleaned
	(in a parking lot) (in a car-wash)
2nd evening:	bodies dirtied with jam
	bodies buried in mounds at the sea edge
	bodies cleaned by the tide

(Kaprow 1966a: 10)

Soap is defined in a double movement, as Kaprow draws the participant into a network of related and often thematically linked activities
yet disperses these activities in order to call its formal frame as a work
into question. Indeed, the activities for *Soap* are not only dispersed, but
are frequently embedded into everyday circumstances, where 'the work'
might bleed out into the private associations of individual participants.
The soiling of clothes, Kaprow suggests 'makes the cleansing of [. . .]
clothes inescapably personal' (Kaprow 1966a: 11). Where cars are taken
to a car wash, Kaprow instructs participants to disguise their performance
in rituals of the everyday, noting that 'one should have this done as
though nothing were out of the ordinary. Any questions should be
answered in as noncommittal a way as possible' (Kaprow 1966a: 11).
Here, in fact, Kaprow works to engage the viewer in a vacillation
between places, as her performed practices are imbricated with *everyday*
rituals, events, and circumstances.

Through these strategies, Kaprow works to transpose Higgins'
concept of intermedia to the relationship between practice and place.
Where, Higgins argues, the happening 'is best defined in terms of what

it is not' (Higgins 1969: 29), Kaprow's happenings 'for performers only' seek to position the viewer-participant's activities between an unfolding artwork and everyday activity. Thus, the viewer's activity *in* the work might force attention *outward*, pressing toward its dissolution into actions, contexts and encounters which constitute its site and cannot be contained, figured, or represented. Writing of 'The Education of the Un-Artist' in 1971, Kaprow remarked that

> Intermedia implies fluidity and simultaneity of roles. Where art is only one of several possible functions a situation might have, it loses its privileged status and becomes, so to speak, a lowercase attribute. The intermedial response can be applied to anything.
>
> (Kaprow 1993c: 105)

It follows that in this ambiguity, where the relationship between 'virtual' and 'real' spaces is continually under review, Kaprow strives to produce a crisis for the limits and borders of the work. Indeed, here, Kaprow actively seeks to break down the specifics of his own work in favour of that which its *abolition* might reveal. Thus, writing on 'Impurity' in 1963, Kaprow remarks that 'Not only the painter's means but also the art object itself should evaporate through a process of mutual annihilation. From this destruction of particulars something of considerably greater importance would be unlocked' (Kaprow 1993b: 30).

It is in this context that Kaprow's well-known 'rules of thumb' for the creation of a happening, first published in 1966, work to exacerbate the problem of locating and so defining and resolving the work. Where, Kaprow states, 'audiences should be eliminated entirely' (Kaprow 1966: 195), these rubrics are designed to work against the viewer-participant's capacity to establish firm or fixed oppositions between the perform-ance and its contexts. Positioning the participant as arbiter of the work's limits, Kaprow states that, in determining the basis of the happening, '*the source of themes, materials, actions, and the relationships between them are to be derived from any place or period* except *from the arts, their derivatives, and their milieu'* (Kaprow 1966: 189). It is this impulse, too, that leads Kaprow to sites outside the conventional places of art viewing. He states that:

> *The performance of a Happening should take place over several widely*
> *spaced, sometimes moving and changing locales* [. . .] by gradually
> widening the distances between the events within a Happening.
> [. . .] in several rooms or floors of an apartment house where
> some of the activities are out of touch with each other; then on
> more than one street; then in different but proximate cities;
> finally all round the globe.
>
> (Kaprow 1966: 190)

Under these strictures, Kaprow's happenings approach specific sites in a series of challenges to the frames in which its limits would be established. Indeed, it is by stretching the perceptual frame of a work to breaking point, and permitting an incursion and ritualising of everyday activity *in performance*, that Kaprow attempts to provoke a situation in which 'art and life are not simply commingled' and where 'the identity of each is uncertain' (Kaprow 1966: 189). At this point, Kaprow supposes, where the limits and so the formal identity of the work are *unclear*, then 'the very materials, the environment, the activity of the people in the environment, are the primary images, not the secondary ones [. . .] there is an absolute flow between event and environment' (Kaprow and Schechner 1968: 154).

Here, then, Kaprow attempts to open the work of art to its own erasure and so to a breaking down towards *site*. It is this effort that Kaprow signals, finally, in these rubrics, stressing that throughout the performance, '*[t]he line between art and life should be kept as fluid, and perhaps indistinct, as possible.* [. . .] Something will always happen at this juncture' (Kaprow 1966: 188–9).

Where Kaprow's happenings 'for performers only' work toward a collapse of the opposition between an abstract framework and the everyday activities in which the work is acted out, Claes Oldenburg's treatment of a '"real" place' as if it were 'itself an object' (Oldenburg 1965: 200) worked to mediate one specific site through another. For *The Store* (1961–2), Oldenburg established a 'real store' at 107 East Second Street, New York, between December 1961 and January 1962, where he kept a stock of approximately 120 everyday objects of all kinds recast in a variety of materials and offered for sale. Here, Oldenburg suggests, *The Store*, as 'artwork', derives its form from the imperatives of the 'real store' it inhabits. Indeed, in this respect, Oldenburg draws attention to his affinity with Kaprow, emphasising that 'the only reason I have taken up Happenings is because I wanted to experiment with total space or surrounding space' (Oldenburg, Lichtenstein and Warhol 1966: 22). Stressing *The Store's* form, as distinct from its commercial function, Oldenburg argues that his arrangement of elements may be 'called a store because like a store it is a collection of objects randomly placed in space' (Oldenburg 1967: 51). Furthermore, in installing these objects in a *functioning*, ostensibly 'non-art' space, Oldenburg suggests,

> I have wanted to imitate my act of perceiving them, which is why they are shown as fragments (in the field of seeing), in different scale to one another, in a form surrounding me (and the spectator), and in accumulation rather than in some imposed design. And the effect is: I have made my own Store.
>
> (Oldenburg 1967: 26)

As a result of this dispersal, Oldenburg concludes, the form of *The Store* 'is not so much environmental as fragmental [. . .] You are to imagine the missing, that is, what is called negative space or absent material, counts for something' (Oldenburg 1967: 49). Here, Oldenburg characterises *The Store* as an incursion into precisely that space which, Kaprow suggests, 'is not palpable as such' (Kaprow 1993: 6), where the viewer will encounter the object's occupation of, and uses in, 'real' space.

In *The Store*, then, as Oldenburg suggests of his other site-specific work, '*The gallery becomes a specific place*' (Oldenburg 1973: 9), a place which, Oldenburg argues in its documentation, 'tries to overcome the

sense of guilt connected with money' and where there is 'no separation between commerce and art' (Oldenburg 1967: 52). In its operation
as a 'real store', however, '*The Store* will be constantly supplied with
new objects' (Oldenburg 1967: 16), and, in this respect, not only does
the gallery *act out* the store, but the store *acts out* the gallery. Indeed,
The Store plays on and through the *difference* between these sites. Thus,
Oldenburg emphasises, '[t]he aim of putting the store in an actual neigh-
bourhood is to *contrast* it to the actual object [. . .] not as might be
thought in neorealist terms to point up similarities' (*sic*) (Oldenburg
1967: 81). Indeed, where *The Store* functions in this relationship of
difference, so the practices in which it is defined come to operate in *more
than one specific place*. It follows that where *The Store* acts as a 'real'
(functioning) store *and* a 'real' (functioning) gallery, so Oldenburg
becomes salesman *and* artist, the visitor customer *and* viewer, and the
object commercial product *and* artwork. Indeed, Oldenburg extends this
duality toward everyday incidents and events at *The Store*, which in turn
enter into performance. Alongside an 'Inventory of the Store' for
December 1961 listing 107 objects for sale, Oldenburg specifies '13
Incidents at the Store', including:

> A customer enters
> Something is bought
> Something is returned
> It costs too much
> A bargain!
> Someone is hired. (someone is fired.)
> The founders. How they struggled.
> Inventory
> Fire sale
> Store closed on acct of death in family
>
> (*sic*) (Oldenburg 1967: 19)

The re-framing of such events reflects *The Store's* multiple function,
not only as store and gallery, but also as the 'Ray Gun Theater' for a

series of events of January 1962, in which Oldenburg sought to define '[a] theatre of action or of things' which might 'present in events what the Store presents in objects' (Oldenburg 1967: 80). Here, Oldenburg suggests, like his other Happenings, the 'audience is considered an object and its behaviours as events, along with the rest' (Oldenburg 1965: 202), with the result that, after Kaprow, 'spectators are both in the "gallery" and in the work' (Oldenburg 1973: 146–7). Here *The Store* articulates its site as *restless* and *mobile*, in a mode of work which Oldenburg characterises as 'always on its way between one point and another' (Oldenburg 1967: 51). Finally, it is in this movement that *The Store* maps its sites, always deferring, in practice, from one place to another.

Where Kaprow and Oldenburg approach the site by testing the work's location, limits, and stability, Wolf Vostell developed his 'dé-coll/age happenings' toward a collapse of the terms of the work into the viewer's encounter with its site. Vostell's performance derived its form from his early 'dé-coll/age' presentations: images derived from a dé-coll/age process, which Vostell defines as to 'unpaste, tear off' (Vostell 1966: 90), applied to 'found', commercially produced posters. In this respect, Vostell's early work had a clear affinity with *affichiste* and junk art by artists such as Raymond Hains and John Chamberlain, where found images and materials, including 'collages from the street' and torn posters, were presented in ways informed by Abstract Expressionist and tachiste painting (Hapgood 1994: 45). In Vostell's dé-coll/age, however, the image is produced in a degrading or destruction, rather than juxtaposition, of found materials. Where, like Kaprow, Vostell positioned his audience as 'participants and performers instead of spectators' (Vostell 1968: 2), the dé-coll/age process extended formal and thematic concerns with processes of destruction, and in doing so became an instrument in the viewer's encounter with 'everyday' events. In setting out the 'Genesis and Iconography of my Happenings' in an 'action-lecture' given at the university of Heidelberg in June 1967, Vostell recalled that, in this development,

I felt a growing necessity to incorporate whatever I
saw/heard/felt/ into my paintings [. . .] what fascinated me were
the symptoms & radiations of a development in my environment
in which destruction, decomposition & change were the strongest
elements – I realized that constructive elements don/t exist in
life at all, they are all intermediate phases of destruction – life is
dé-coll/age – as the body builds up and grows, it wears out at the
same time – permanent destruction.

(sic) (Vostell 1968: 4)

Here the dé-coll/age happening effects an opening to its sites by
calling its own framework and identity into question. Emphasising 'no
retreat from but into reality' (Vostell 1968: 1), Vostell stresses that in
the dé-coll/age happening 'I use the actual locations where the events
would normally occur: airports/highways/car dumps/slaughter houses/
multilevel garages/supermarkets etc.' (Vostell 1968: 14). In this effort
'to erase in order to see and let others see clearly' (Vostell 1966: 40),
Vostell concludes, 'my happenings and events are frames of reference
for experiencing the present' (Vostell 1966: 2). Here, then, the boundary
between the happening and its location, between the work and its place,
threatens to disappear. In Cityrama 1 (1961) in Cologne, for example,
Vostell organised 'a walk through the city with the audience, to bombed
sites/backyards/scrapyards/etc. where I declared as art found objects, or
the particular condition of a site or building, or an event, or an entire
environment' (Vostell 1968: 12).

In this 'permanent realistic demonstration [. . .] at 26 sites' (Vostell
1966: 15–16), Vostell's tour directed attention toward 'life and realistic
actions and occurrences declared to be de-coll/age works of art' (Vostell
1966: 15), prompting the participant-viewers to:

walk   listen   speak
1 – ruin at maximinen strasse
    (entrance on dom strasse)
2 – ruin at maximinen strasse

(entrance on dom strasse)
3 – ruin at maximinen strasse
(entrance on dom strasse)
4 – ruin at maximinen strasse
(entrance on dom strasse)

(Vostell 1966: 15)

Defined, Vostell suggests, in 'the sum total of events and the distance between the single events' (Vostell 1968: 1), and prompting 'chaotic situations', which, Vostell states, 'cannot always be resolved' (Vostell 1966: 2), the dé-coll/age happening confronts the viewer with actions, events, sites, or instructions, whose place *within* a work is uncertain. Indeed, here, on being invited to be 'actively engaged in a series of events that have not been rehearsed' (Vostell 1968: 14), in a mode of work in which 'each happening exposes itself to the banality of the viewer or participant' (Vostell 1968: 7), the participant may simply find themselves, under the frame of Vostell's work, *at* a given place.

These attempts to displace the viewer-participant *into* the site have strong affinities to the Situationist International's attempts to map the 'psychogeographical relief' of the city in a technique adopted from Dadaist practice (Plant 1992: 58). Thus, writing of 'The Theory of the Derive' in 1956, Guy Debord announced that '[a]mong the various situationist methods is the *derive* [literally: 'drifting'], a technique of transient passage through various ambiences' (Debord 1981: 50). Here, 'one or more persons during a certain period drop their usual motives for movement and action, their relations, their leisure and work activities, and let themselves be drawn by the attractions of the terrain and the encounters they find there' (Debord 1981: 50). Among the means of provoking a sensitivity, openness, or sense of *drift*, Debord suggests, is the 'possible rendezvous' where

The subject is invited to come alone to a specified place at a specified time. He is freed from the bothersome obligations of the ordinary rendezvous since there is no-one to wait for. But

since this 'possible rendezvous' has brought him without warning
to a place he may or may not know, he observes the
surroundings. It may be that the same spot has been specified for
a 'possible rendezvous' for someone else whose identity he has no
way of knowing. Since he may never have even seen the other
person before, he will be incited to start up conversations with
various passers-by. He may meet no-one, or he may by chance
meet the person who has arranged the 'possible rendezvous.' In
any case, particularly if the time and place have been well chosen,
the subject's use of time will take an unexpected turn. He may
even telephone someone else who doesn't know where the first
'possible rendezvous' has taken him, in order to ask for another
one to be specified.

(Debord 1981: 53)

For Vostell, approaching the complexities of maintaining a work while
being in the site, the dé-coll/age happening may embrace an event analogous to the possible rendezvous, where the invitation to act out the
work displaces the viewer's place and purpose, in favour of a height-
ened attention to 'found' events and sites. In this respect, these
happenings look toward the 'pre-cartographic' (Jameson 1991: 51) experience Jameson identifies with Lynch's phenomenological mapping of
the city: an *acting out* of the site, a mapping caught in the moment
of its *being performed*.

These approaches to site elaborate a position consistent with
Smithson's proposal that 'the site is a place where the piece should be
but isn't' (Bear and Sharp 1996: 249–50). Yet where Smithson's
Non-Sites foreground the site's *absences*, these prompts toward
phenomenological engagements with found sites look toward another
possibility. Thus, these works by Kaprow, Oldenburg, and Vostell
prompt exchanges between an artwork and its site in a which a specificity to site arises in the promise that the viewer's own engagement
with *this place* might leave the work behind.

Space as Map and Memory: Meredith Monk

The development of Meredith Monk's site-specific work, while grounded in her rigorous dance training (Koenig 1976: 52), was strongly shaped by the exchanges between music, dance and visual art defining the new performance emerging in New York from the early 1960s. During her dance studies at Sarah Lawrence College, Monk had participated in Merce Cunningham's first series of dance workshops in the summer of 1962 (Banes 1978: 72) and periodically attended performances of the Judson Dance Theatre in New York City. In 1964 she moved to Manhattan where, Sally Banes records, 'besides choreographing and dancing her own works, she performed in Happenings, off-Broadway plays, and other dance works' (Banes 1978: 4). Yet, while drawing on the work of the Judson Dance Theatre, Monk also reacted against the formal austerity of these reactions against Modern American dance. Thus, Monk's early work engaged with the overt theatricality of Happenings by artists such as Robert Whitman, Al Hansen, and Carolee Schneemann, as well as the inter-disciplinary practices associated with Fluxus. In 1965 Monk collaborated with the Fluxus artists Dick Higgins, Alison Knowles and Ay-O on a realisation of the Dada performance *Relaché* for the New York avant-garde festival of 1965 (Jowitt 1997: 4). In the same year, she performed in Higgins' *The Tart, or, Miss America* and *The Celestials* (Hansen 1965: 21) and in Al Hansen's *Silver City for Andy Warhol* (Koenig 1976: 12). Monk herself recalls working with the poet Jackson Mac Low (Bear and Monk 1997: 83) who had collaborated with Cage in the untitled event of 1952. For Monk, the exchanges between visual art, dance, theatre, poetry, and film which underpinned this work evidently provided the basis for her engagement in a new mode of performance, which she recalled as 'A nonlinear dramatic mosaic that incorporated film, dance, music, and image. The people who were closest to it formally were Whitman and [Robert] Morris' theatre pieces. They'd worked with images as a primary element, rather than a movement' (Bear and Monk 1997: 84).

In this context, Monk's early choreographic concepts found their counterpart in her approach to specific sites. In her earliest published notes on her work, for the dance *Portable* realised at the Judson Church Theatre in May 1966, Monk characterises her choreographic concern for transition in terms of the map's absence from its object. Monk records that

> I started thinking about the idea of residue. Something left behind or coming after a process has ended. [. . .] The past and present in one piece. A map. A map is always used as a guide, a reference *before* (sometimes during) travel. In this piece, the map would be a continuous process (during the piece) and a residue of the process of the entire piece.
>
> (Jowitt 1997: 18)

It is a set of concerns elaborated explicitly in her major site-specific work, *Juice* of 1969, in which mapping provides a mechanism and metaphor for the work. Performed in three parts in three different locations over a period of a month and a half, the 'guiding concept' of *Juice*, Siri Engberg notes in Monk's documentation of this work, is the 'close-up' or zoom-lens. In Part One, then, realised by eighty-five performers in the Solomon R. Guggenheim Museum, New York, Monk used 'the whole building as a kind of sculptural experience for the audience' (Bernhardt *et al.* 1994), deploying performers on the spiralling ramps defining the Museum's central gallery and, she later recalled, 'using the sound of that space, which has almost a half-second delay' (Strickland 1997: 137). At the same time, the Guggenheim performance provided for an intimacy between performers and audience. Monk's programme notes to the audience for Section II of the Guggenheim performance record:

> Audience walking on ramps
> Performers in the bays, alcoves,
> stairways along the outside edge of

the ramps
This is a 45 minute interval consisting of
13 simultaneous events distributed on the
six ramp levels of the museum.

(Monk 1969)

While the audience are invited to move at will around the ramp levels,
so these events play continuously, in the manner of an exhibition.
Subsequently, Monk's notes conclude, the performance ends with the
audience on the ramp looking down to the performers on the ground
floor (Monk 1969). Part Two of *Juice* was realised one month later at
Barnard College's Minor Latham Playhouse in a systematic translation
of one site and event into another, yet a translation in which, Banes
recalls,

> everything had diminished. At the entrance to the theatre, a child
> sat on a rockinghorse – a smaller echo of the woman who rode a
> horse down Fifth Avenue as the audience waited outside the
> Guggenheim for part one. Inside the theatre [. . .] characters gave
> information about themselves in recitatives, and performed real-
> life actions [. . .] Many more elements from the first part were
> rearranged and shrunk in this presentation.
>
> (Banes 1978: 5)

While the Minor Latham Playhouse provides an ostensibly more
intimate space, its proscenium arch introduces a new kind of formality
and distance. Part Three, realised one week later at Monk's loft in
Manhattan, consisted of an exhibition of objects and costumes from the
earlier parts of the piece. Amidst these objects, the four principal
performers of *Juice* were framed in close-up on large television screens
positioned on the floor, recounting on video-tape their experiences of
working on the piece. Here, Banes recalls, 'though one could even smell
the sweat of the costumes, the performers remained totally remote,
once-removed by the video screen' (Banes 1978: 5–6).

As *Juice* plays out the 'close-up', so its three parts trace out a process in which one space and site acts as the map and memory of another. In doing so, the piece approaches its sites in a double movement, in which, as the elements of performance move into close-up, so the sites and events of which they are an index move farther away. Indeed, in the relationship between work and site, *Juice* plays out the terms Monk describes for *Portable*, where 'the map would be a continuous process (during the piece)' and in which 'material and transition would go on simultaneously' (Jowitt 1997: 18). Furthermore, in its transitions from site to site, *Juice* traces out the map's paradoxical relationship to its object.

These concerns are reflected elsewhere in Monk's site-specific works which frequently unfold in a disjunctive mapping of one set of terms over another. For *Blueprint* of 1967, Banes recalls, 'spectators sat outside a building to view events in windows. Some of the events were live, some filmed, some a combination of projected film image on identical live action' (Banes 1978: 12). As the piece unfolded, 'the audience moved from place to place to view activities' (Banes 1978: 5), so extending the implicit invitation to negotiate between live and filmed activities and its sites. Subsequently, 'the audience returned a month after the first section was given, to see the second part' (Banes 1978: 5), so incorporating memory and residue into this negotiation. *Needlebrain Lloyd and the Systems Kid* of 1970 extended this process in an explicit *writing over* of a large outdoor space through the conceits of film in order to produce 'a live movie'. In doing so, the piece sets an explicitly limiting mechanism against the 'limitlessness' (Bernhardt *et al.* 1994) of the space it attempts to organise, loosening the boundaries of the work as it displaces its own conventions. *Vessel*, originally performed in 1971, extends this opening up of the work to its sites again, as it plays out a reversal of the close-up underpinning *Juice*, progressing from Monk's loft, to the Performing Garage in SoHo, to the Wooster Street parking lot.

In these various ways, Monk's site-specific work consistently presents itself *in movement*, where the relationship between performance and its places is a disjunctive one, is in transition, or calls on memory. Such concerns with process and transition reflect, again, Peter Eisenman's account of the effect of the site's *absences*. In understanding this effect, Eisenman suggests, we might consider

> the difference between a *moving arrow* and a still arrow [. . .] if a picture of each were taken and compared, they would be virtually indistinguishable. What distinguishes the moving arrow from the still one is that it contains where it has been and where it is going, i.e., it has a memory and an immanence that are not present to the observer of the photograph; they are essential *absences*.*
>
> (Eisenman 1986: 5–6)

In the rhythms of appearance and disappearance, anticipation and memory in which these various *mappings* of site are acted out, this site-specific work, from Smithson to Oldenburg to Monk, reflects on a contemporary space or place 'which can only be represented *in motion*' (Jameson 1991: 45). Indeed, these site-specific works can be characterised precisely in their *acting out* of a process, which, like its object, is continually 'on the way between one point and another' (Oldenburg 1967: 51).

* I am indebted to Gabriella Giannachi for directing me toward this quotation.

Ten Feet and Three Quarters of an Inch of Theatre

A Documentation of a site-specific Theatre Work

Instructions to The Reader

On the following twelve pages is a graphic documentation of the site-specific theatre work Tri Bywyd, performed by Brith Gof in a forest in west Wales in October 1995.

In a number of significant ways, this documentation, though thorough, is incomplete.

The limitations of page by page turning, of monochrome print and of size - all necessary to link format and academic worth - have led the writer to adopt a set of conceits that make this, the thing that the reader holds in her hand, an unfinished document.

Should she choose to extend the documentation, to complete the process, then the reader will:

1

photocopy each of the twelve pages to an enlargement of 200%

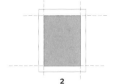

2

cut away the margins around each page

3

place the pages in sequence next to each other and tape them together to create a document that will be one foot three inches high and ten feet and three quarters of an inch long

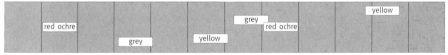

4

clarify the confusion caused by black/white/greyness by introducing colour onto the areas indicated

Alternatively, the reader might prefer to retain the charged erotics of incompletion by leaving things as they are - forever unfinished.

Clifford McLucas
Artistic Director
Brith Gof

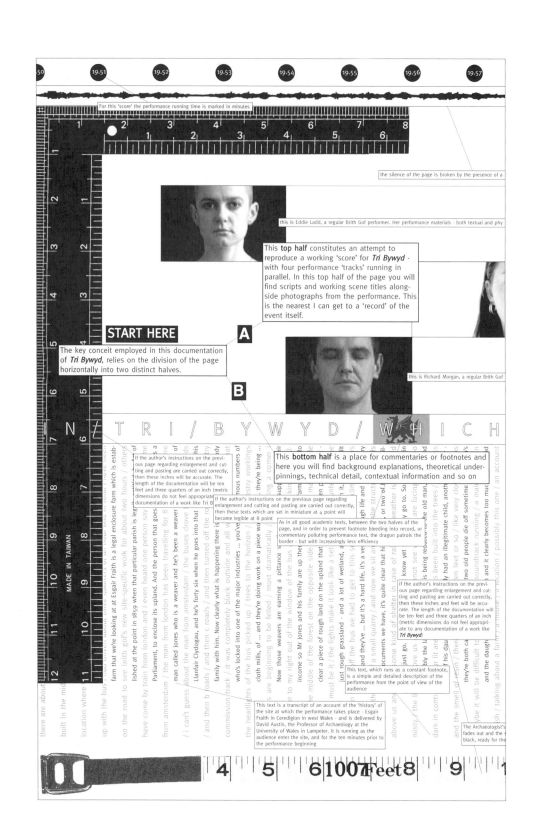

19.51 19.52 19.53 19.54 19.55 19.56 19.57

For this 'score' the performance running time is marked in minutes

the silence of the page is broken by the presence of a

this is Eddie Ladd, a regular Brith Gof performer. Her performance materials - both textual and phy

This **top half** constitutes an attempt to reproduce a working 'score' for *Tri Bywyd* - with four performance 'tracks' running in parallel. In this top half of the page you will find scripts and working scene titles alongside photographs from the performance. This is the nearest I can get to a 'record' of the event itself.

START HERE

A

The key conceit employed in this documentation of *Tri Bywyd*, relies on the division of the page horizontally into two distinct halves.

B

this is Richard Morgan, a regular Brith Gof

I N / T R I / B Y W Y D / W H I C H

MADE IN TAIWAN

This **bottom half** is a place for commentaries or footnotes and here you will find background explanations, theoretical underpinnings, technical detail, contextual information and so on

If the author's instructions on the previous page regarding enlargement and cutting and pasting are carried out correctly, then these inches will be accurate. The length of the documentation will be ten feet and three quarters of an inch (metric dimensions do not feel appropriate to any documentation of a work like Tri B

If the author's instructions on the previous page regarding enlargement and cutting and pasting are carried out correctly, then these texts which are set in miniature at 4 point will become legible at 8 point

As in all good academic texts, between the two halves of the page, and in order to prevent footnote bleeding into record, or commentary polluting performance text, the dragon patrols the border - but with increasingly less efficiency

If the author's instructions on the previous page regarding enlargement and cutting and pasting are carried out correctly, then these inches and feet will be accurate. The length of the documentation will be ten feet and three quarters of an inch (metric dimensions do not feel appropriate to any documentation of a work like *Tri Bywyd*)

farm that we're looking at at Esgair Fraith is a legal enclosure farm which is established at the point in 1859 when that particular parish is leg on the road to see brith gof's new site-specific work for about two hours / others have come by train from london and i even heard one person say Parliament, to enclose its upland. And the person that goes from amsterdam / the man from london has been travelling for 8 man called Jones who is a weaver and he's been a weaver / i can't guess about the man from amsterdam / the buses drove Llanfair Clydogau, and he's forty six when he goes into that / and then b oads / and then c roads / and then turned off the ro family with him. Now clearly what is happening there is the headlights of the bus picked up / trees to the horizon / cloth mills, of ... and they're doing work on a piece wo commission track / it was completely black outside and all w who's locked into one of the major industries ... you've

Now those weavers are earning a pittance to my right out of the window of the bus income so Mr Jones and his family are up the middle of the forest on the opposite side clear a piece of rough land on the upland that must be it / the lights make it look like a set just rough grassland - and a lot of wetland, a ff the bus we had to get to this s and they've ... but it's a hard life, it's a ve a small quarry / and now we sit an some kind of shelter in case of ra

This text, which runs as a constant footnote, is a simple and detailed description of the performance from the point of view of the audience

This text is a transcript of an account of the 'history' of the site at which the performance takes place - Esgair Fraith in Ceredigion in west Wales - and is delivered by David Austin, the Professor of Archaeology at the University of Wales in Lampeter. It is running as the audience enter the site, and for the ten minutes prior to the performance beginning

The Archaeologist's fades out and the black, ready for the

4 5 6 100 7 Feet 8 9 1

BLUE

all scene numbers

these are Grett and Tom Jenkins. Regular performers in the Radio Ceredigion 'soap' **Bontlwyd** broadcast twice daily from Felinfach. Tom and

continuous soundtrack

During the blackout, the soundtrack for the performance begins

YELLOW

CA

sical - is developed from the story of Sarah Jacob - the Welsh fasting Girl. Her texts and scene titles run on this track - number two

Occasionally, items will be highlighted and given a colour. This is to seek to overcome the severe limitations of documentation of a work like **Tri Bywyd** in twelve small monochrome pages. The reader/user may choose to colour these items on his/her full size copy

this is Gwenllian Rhys, a regular Brith Gof performer. Her material - both textual and physical - is developed from the story of the murder of the Cardiff prostitute Linette White. Her texts and scene

Structurally, **Tri Bywyd** is made up of 39 two minute scenes - three groups of thirteen. Within each group of thirteen, a death occurs.

to be used on every page - thereby cutting the document into two halves
RED

performer. Richard's material - both textual and physical - is developed in response to the three lives above. His texts and scene titles run on this track - number four

/ T R A N S L A T E S   I N T O / E

The Performance begins

In Scene One, the site - which has been in darkness - is revealed. The five performers are in position, but are immobile

During the thirty nine scenes of **Tri Bywyd** three deaths occur. These are marked by the black and yellow diagonals. This first one is a re-enactment of the murder of Linette White, and occurs four minutes into the performance

In Scene Two, Tom, the elderly man, begins to move from the rear of the site towards the audience removing sheets that are draped over numerous installations

In Scene Three, two performers re-enact the murder of Linette White in one of the two houses - moving from 'front door' through 'hallway' up 'stairs' and ending at first floor level in the 'bedroom'. The other performers slowly turn on the spot

In Scene Four......

In Scene Five....

see descriptive text

The site of Esgair Fraith is slowly revealed - to show that the audience is seated on slightly higher ground, looking down on a number of ruined buildings, with two steel tube structures set within these ruins beneath a canopy of softwoods and amongst the convoluted branches of the hardwoods

description slowly site lights fade to performance to begin

she either sells up or gets out and leaves, and the next people we see are a young couple, also who come from the local community who take it on as a farming enterprise only. Their name is Davies and we see them then through the Great War into the 1920's. In 1926 Mrs Davies dies and the old man goes on farming until

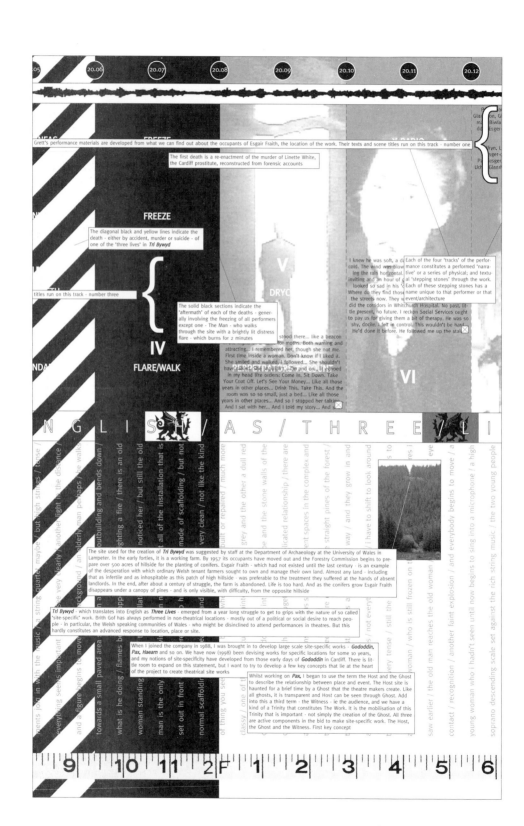

Grett's performance materials are developed from what we can find out about the occupants of Esgair Fraith, the location of the work. Their texts and scene titles run on this track · number one

The first death is a re-enactment of the murder of Linette White, the Cardiff prostitute, reconstructed from forensic accounts

FREEZE

The diagonal black and yellow lines indicate the death - either by accident, murder or suicide - of one of the 'three lives' in *Tri Bywyd*

titles run on this track · number three

The solid black sections indicate the 'aftermath' of each of the deaths - gener- ally involving the freezing of all performers except one - The Man - who walks through the site with a brightly lit distress flare - which burns for 2 minutes

IV

FLARE/WALK

V

DRYC...

VI

I knew he was soft, a d... cold. The wind was blow... ing the rain horizontal... inviting and an hour of g... looked so sad in his '... Where do they find thos... the streets now. They w... did the corridors in Whitchurch Hospital. No past, lit- tle present, no future. I reckon Social Services ought to pay us for giving them a bit of therapy. He was so shy, docile. I felt in control. This wouldn't be hard. He'd done it before. He followed me up the stai...

Each of the four 'tracks' of the perfor- mance constitutes a performed 'narra- tive' or a series of physical; and textu- al 'stepping stones' through the work. Each of these stepping stones has a name unique to that performer or that event/architecture

...stood there... like a beacon ...for moths. Both warning and attracting... I remembered her, though she not me. First time inside a woman. Don't know if I liked it. She smiled and walked, I followed... She shouldn't have ...done... On and on... all echoed in my head like orders: Come In. Sit Down. Take Your Coat Off. Let's See Your Money... Like all those years in other places... Drink This. Take This. And the room was so so small, just a bed... Like all those years in other places... And so I stopped her talking... And I sat with her... And I told my story... And s...

N G L I S H / A S / T H R E E L I

See very clearly / another light in the distance /

background / an elderly man perhaps / he walks

events join in with the music / a string quarte maybe / but high strings / tense /

outbuilding and bends down

lighting a fire / there is an old

noticed her / but still the old

all of the installation that is

made of scaffolding / but not

very clean / not like the kind

built or repaired / much more

grey and the other a dull red

and the stone walls of the

...cated relationship / there are

...ent spaces in the complex and

straight pines of the forest /

way / and they grow in and

I have to shift to look around

The site used for the creation of *Tri Bywyd* was suggested by staff at the Department of Archaeology at the University of Wales in Lampeter. In the early forties, it is a working farm. By 1957 its occupants have moved out and the Forestry Commission begins to pre- pare over 500 acres of hillside for the planting of conifers. Esgair Fraith - which had not existed until the last century - is an example of the desperation with which ordinary Welsh tenant farmers sought to own and manage their own land. Almost any land - including that as infertile and as inhospitable as this patch of high hillside - was preferable to the treatment they suffered at the hands of absent landlords. In the end, after about a century of struggle, the farm is abandoned. Life is too hard. And as the conifers grow Esgair Fraith disappears under a canopy of pines - and is only visible, with difficulty, from the opposite hillside

Tri Bywyd - which translates into English as *Three Lives* - emerged from a year long struggle to get to grips with the nature of so called 'site-specific' work. Brith Gof has always performed in non-theatrical locations - mostly out of a political or social desire to reach peo- ple - in particular, the Welsh speaking communities of Wales - who might be disinclined to attend performances in theatres. But this hardly constitutes an advanced response to location, place or site.

When I joined the company in 1988, I was brought in to develop large scale site-specific works - *Gododdin*, *Pax*, *Haearn* and so on. We have now (1998) been devising works for specific locations for some 10 years, and my notions of site-specificity have developed from those early days of *Gododdin* in Cardiff. There is lit- tle room to expand on this statement, but I want to try to develop a few key concepts that lie at the heart of the project to create theatrical site works

Whilst working on *Pax*, I began to use the term the Host and the Ghost to describe the relationship between place and event. The Host site is haunted for a brief time by a Ghost that the theatre makers create. Like all ghosts, it is transparent and Host can be seen through Ghost. Add into this a third term - the Witness - ie the audience, and we have a kind of a Trinity that constitutes The Work. It is the mobilisation of this Trinity that is important - not simply the creation of the Ghost. All three are active components in the bid to make site-specific work. The Host, the Ghost and the Witness. First key concept

everything seems important

and a figure begins to move

towards a small paved area

what is he doing / flames b...

woman standing

man is the only

set out in front

normal scaffoldi...

of thing you see

classy / one of t...

...s to

...res i

eye

i / not everyt...

...very tense / still the

woman / who is still frozen on t...

saw earlier / the old man reaches the old woman

contact / recognition / another faint explosion / another faint...

young woman who i hadn't seen until now begins to sing into a microphone / a high

soprano descending scale set against the rich string music / the two young people

ne, Pant-y-fedwen, s
anrhyd, Lluest Ucha,
Pantresger, Blaenp
ddu, Esger Llanfer, L
Brith, Mo'llfy

GWEU

ether Brith, Llether
ddu, Graig-ddu, Penge
Biwla, Esgeirman,
yd, Glanrafon, Preto
fedwen, Pentreba

The Welsh Language. Yr Iaith Gymraeg. Where to begin - to explain the significance of working in Wales in the Welsh and English languages - to describe the astonishingly high level of debate in Wales around themes of identity, culture. location, centre and periphery, colonialism, imperialism etc etc - to persuade the monoglot English reader that to live and work bilingually - to flip from language to language, from identity to identity, from one window on the world to another - is the most exciting, negotiated process I can imagine - to persuade that same reader that bi (and plurl) lingualism is a state of affairs for most nations and that Wales is accordingly the most contemporary small European nation in these islands - and that a Britain characterised as one thing - as, in fact, England - is a most desperately boring and regressive notion - and that..... and that.... and that....

FE:
Ma'lfro... Llether Brith, Lle'ger Ganu, Esger Llanfer...
A soundtrack runs through the whole piece, and all voices are delivered through microphones and pa
system. At no point, in this 'natural' landscape is a 'natural' or acoustic sound delivered by the work

Ucha, Glanrhyd, Glanrafon, Pretoria, Sarn-llys, Pant-y-
fedwen, Pentrebanne.
HI:
Be' ti'n neud?
FE YN EI FLAEN, HEB GOLLI RHYTHM
HI:
Be' ti'n neud?
FE YN EI FLAEN
HI:
Be' ti'n neud? Be' ti'n neud?
FE YN EI FLAEN
HI:
Be'ti'n neud...
Y DDAU:
ER MWYN POPETH!
SAIB
HI: [YN DAWEL]
Er mwyn popeth; Beth wyt ti'n neud?
DIM YMATEB
HI: [YN DAWEL (AWN]
Beth wyt ti'n 'neud?
YN Y PEN-DRAW:
FE:
Ti'n gwbod beth fi'n neud.
HI:
Odw-i?
FE:
Wyt. Mae'n digwydd digon amaL
HI:

Druan. Am faint fyddi di fyn'na heno, tybed. Cyn i'r
... gwbod.
... ar ol nôs,
... lo ynddo'l.

Fi wedi dod i wbod. A fi'n gwbod am y gole hefyd.
Fi'n gwbod am y gwyfyn sy'n gaeth yn dy fula-
berfedd. Edrych am ole Pentre-banne, Esger-ddu a'r
gweddill i gyd. Ond twyll yw e, ti'n gwbod. Twyllo dy
hunan wyt ti, ti'n gwbod. Ti'n gwbod am brion ble
bynnag bydde ti - 'se ti draw ochot-draw'r cwm 'co -
ble bynnag fydde ti mas ar y clos fydde tl. Yn whilo
am y gole. Whilo, whilo, whilo am y gole. Felna [X]

ER

There were no witnesses but everyone had a story. Wanting to be part of it, wanting to be in it. So many stories. A story composed of stories and stories about stories. Only two missing: hers and his. The awful silence at the heart... Mark Grommek, who lived

OOKED AT 2

The only agent of interlinkage between the three lives/worlds is the figure of Richard Morgan, who shifts from world to world and performs a multitude of functions - some which might be interpreted as supportive, some destructive and some 'blank'

Otherwise the orchestration of the three separate 'narratives' is the work of an outside eye or director. The performers. who never meet or interface. are not the creators of 'theatre', and the normal techniques available to them to alter theatrical dynamic, to 'improve' their performances, and so on, are absent

he wants or he'll fuck yo
woman "I haven't got it."

VII

Go-whith.
FE:

Instead. peripheral vision, listening and awareness - a kind of open sensitivity - is the most useful and subtle technique available to performers in this kind of work - over expression or fake energy would be a dis-service to the work - which relies on a symphonic relationship between one person's text, another's action, and a range of other formal 'correspondences'

And it is here - in the spaces between performers, in the spaces between the three lives, in the spaces between the three architectures - that the work begins to emerge. And the means by which the theatre makers might manipulate or control this kind of work are quite different to those that might be employed in other 'object' based theatres.

V E S / T H E / R I C H / R E L A T

The conifers planted by the Forestry Commission blanket the hillside and cut off any views that Esgair Fraith once enjoyed

Beech and sycamore trees originally planted to mark the hedges around the fields close to the house have grown outwards and upwards in convoluted shapes in order to reach the light obscured by the fast growing pines

Timbers have rotted, walls have started to crumble, and stones are covered in vivid green moss

Now these three components of a 'developed' address to site-specific theatre events are, most crucially, not objects. They are constellations of effects, attitudes, ownerships, built materials, histories, firmly held beliefs and so on. They constitute a temporary but unique ecology. Second key concept

Unlike a hand in a glove, the relationship between Host, Ghost and Witness can never be a perfect one. Each will always generate More or Less than is required by the other - leading to conditions of surplus or starvation. Third key concept

Haemorrhaging of location, event and audience into each other might be a key technique in a further advancement of the concept of site-specificity

XIII

The end of the first group of thirteen scenes

PWY SY 'NA?   AROLYG   GOLCHI XIV

You will see that it is a long single storey stone building with a thatched roof. Inside you will see a cow shed, next to the farm servants bedroom, then the kitchen and, finally, the main bedroom, where the event will take place. Onto the rear of this long farm house, there is a lean to consisting of two rooms - a dairy and a scullery - both opening off the main kitchen. You will enter the main bedroom through a door from the kitchen. And this is where it will happen. This is where it always happens. As you enter you will see, on the wall opposite, a fireplace, which has been unused for two years and has been blocked ✕

It was a cold, damp and forbidding place and she was known to hate it. She kept no possessions there but simply used it to earn money from her clients. For occasionally men want sex indoors and some prostitutes keep badly maintained rooms. A squalid place for a squalid business. The small, first floor flat above a betting shop had no electricity and very little furniture. The only light came from the street-lamp outside the window. In the sitting room was a dirty soiled bed - a red divan ... a ... the ... item of furniture. ... ... met her death. Th...

SGWÂR XII

EVAN JACOB a HANNAH JACOB - Parents. Y ddou yngannol 'u tridege. Tenantied ffarm Llethemeuadd-uchaf, ger Lanfihangel-ar-Arth, Sir Gyfyrddin. Rhieni Sarah Jacob, 'The Welsh Fasting Girl'.

MARGARET JACOB - Chwaer Sarah, chwech mlwydd wed. Yn ei bwydo trwy gusannu, falle.

UN, DAU, TRI, PEDWAR, PUMP DOCTOR

YMWELWYR - Yn aros yn y gegin cyn ca'l mynd miwn i'w gweld. Ei thyblo yn saint, yn dod a llyfre iddi ac yn gadael arian ar 'i chest.

JOHN GRIFFITH - Gohebydd a berodd gwahodd wylwyr annibynnol o Guy's Hospital yn Llunden i ddod i setlo'r mater.

PEDAIR NYRS GUY'S HOSPITAL - Sister Elizabeth Clinch a'r nyrsus Sarah Attrick, Sarah Palmer ac Anne Jones, Cymraes.

... ... claf, 10 mlwydd wed yn 1867.

...ach hyd April 1867:
...yn 'i hochor whith
... ag ewyn yn 'i cheg

Since creating the previous large scale work *Haearn*, a work that brings together the myths of Hephaestus and Prometheus, accounts of the development of medical and industrial science, and the personal letters and diaries of Mary Shelley, all operating within a framework of seven overlaid or interpenetrating architectures - I had been keen to investigate the theatrical possibilities inherent in the 'in between' places in theatre - at all levels - place, architecture, text, action. This remains my obsession at the time of writing - and recent pieces such as *Once upon a Time in the West, Hafod - A Life in Eight Great Suites* and *Lla'th (Gwynfyd)* all extend this practice.

Tri Bywyd constitutes an attempt to get to grips with the development of techniques that will bring about a kind of 'theatrical poetics' - the term 'poetics' being used to contrast with terms such as 'documentary' or 'narrative'.

...diagnosed inflammation of the brain

May 1867:
collodd ei gwallt

May hyd October 1867:
Byta'n llai ac yn llai ✕

LOOKING AT XI

I O N S H I P / B E T W E E N / H

Finally, the notion emerges of a **hybrid** between place and action, between architecture and event - Host might be haunted by other ghosts - not of the theatrician's making, and Ghost might also come with an in built Host - a ready made event architecture of its own. Third key concept

Wary of the dangers of such a site as Esgair Fraith becoming 'natural' or 'beautiful' and thus closing down any speculation or problematisation of meaning in the 'natural environment', I decided to import two Ghosts to overlay and interpenetrate Esgair Fraith. These Ghosts are in themselves Hosts for other Ghosts - architectures (houses) carrying their own events (performances)

This notion of event/architecture was central to the development of the ideas for *Tri Bywyd*. My thinking began at about the same time as the details were emerging of Fred and Rose West's activities in their home in 25 Cromwell Terrace in Gloucester in England - where they murdered a number of young people and built their bodies into the fabric of the house. The horror of the domestic - where abuse and diy live side by side - became a thematic concern for me, and I began to think about the hybrid of performance and architecture - event and room - in new ways. I decided to find a site for a work - in the landscape - and that that Host should be haunted by two other Hosts - each with their own Ghosts - ie two event/rooms, two performance architectures, two house/narratives overlaid onto the Host site.

3387
158ha
·39

© Crown Copyright

ESGAIR FRAITH - Ordnance Survey map

The Host site was suggested to us by the staff at the Archaeology Department at the University of Wales in Lampeter

ESGAIR FRAITH - Aerial photograph taken in the 1940's before the forest was planted

Esgair Fraith in the hills above Llanfair Clydogau near Lampeter, is a ruined farmhouse and outbuildings. It had been abandoned in the thirties and eventually bought by the Forestry Commission who planted softwoods to the horizon. These trees eventually grew higher than the buildings of Esgair Fraith and submerged the farm in a green mossy gloom - making it invisible except from a distance where the deciduous trees of the farm's hedges could still be seen against the dark green of the plantation

·194ha

5   6   7   8   9   10   4   2

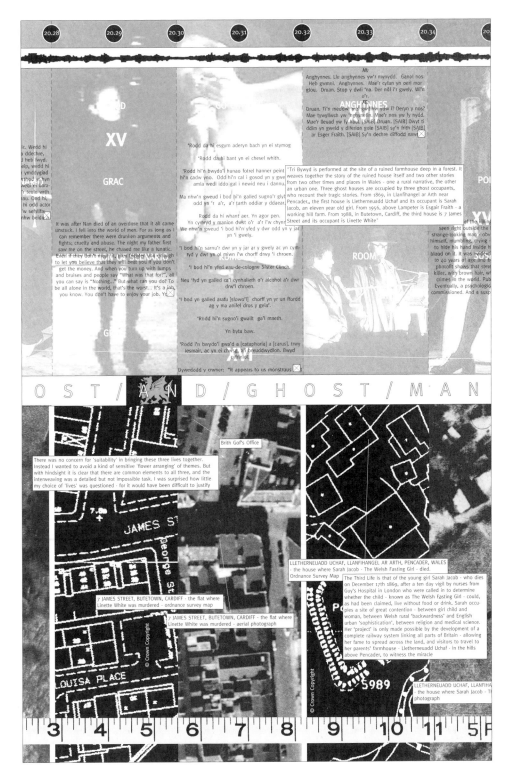

Hi:
Anghynnes. Lle anghynnes yw'r mynydd. Ganol nos.
Heb gwmni. Anghynnes. Mae'r cyfan yn oeri mor
glou. Druan. Stop y dwli 'na. Der nôl i'r gwely. Wi'n
o'r.

ANGHYNNES

Druan. Ti'n meddw mai gwddw ydw i? Deryn y nos?
Mae tywyllwch yw 'nghynefin. Mae'r nos yw fy nydd.
Mae'r lleuad yw fy haul. [SAIB] Druan. [SAIB] Dwy ti
ddim yn gweld y diferion gole [SAIB] sy'n ffrith [SAIB]
ar Esger Fraith. [SAIB] Sy'n dechre diffodd nawr [X]

XV

GRAC

'Rodd da hi esgyrn aderyn bach yn ei stymog

'Rodd da hi bant yn ei chesel whith.

'Rodd hi'n bwydo'i hunao fotrel hanner peint
hi'n cadw yno. Odd hi'n cal i gosod yn y gwel
amla wedi iddo gal i newid neu i dannu.

Ma nhw'n gweud i bod hi'n galled sugno'r glyb
odd yn 'r a'r, a'r tarth oddiar y ddaear.

'Rodd da hi whant aer. Yn agor pen.
Yn cymryd y manion dwst o'r a'r i'w chynn
We nhw'n gweud 'i bod hi'n yfed y dwr odd yn y jar
yn 'i gwely.

'I bod hi'n sarnu'r dwr yn y jar ar y gwely ac yn cymryd y dwr yn ol miwn i'w chorff drwy 'i chroen.

'I bod hi'n yfed eau-de-cologne Sister Clinch.

Neu 'fyd yn galled ca'l cynhalieth o'r alcohol a'r dwr
drw'i chroen.

'I bod yn galled arafu [slowo'l] chorff yn yr un ffordd
ag y ma anifel dros y gela'.

'Rodd hi'n sugno'i gwallt go'l maeth.

Yn byta baw.

'Rodd i'n bwydo'i gwa'd a [cataphoria] a [carus], trwy
iesmair, ac yn ei chwsg, a'i breuddwydion. Bwyd
cyfriniol.

Dywedodd y crwner; "It appears to us monstrous [X]

Ic. Wedd hi
a ddechre,
a heb fwyd.
elp, wedd hi
y ymddygiad
irffed yr hyn
wedi ei bara-
'r teulu with
au. Ond hi,
hi odd actor
'w setyllfa-
nhw beidia [△]

It was after Nan died of an overdose that it all came
unstuck. I fell into the world of men. For as long as I
can remember there were drunken arguments and
fights; cruelty and abuse. The night my father first
saw me on the street, he chased me like a lunatic.
Even if they don't mean it, they frighten you enough
to let you believe that they will beat you if you don't
get the money. And when you turn up with lumps
and bruises and people say "What was that for?", all
you can say is "Nothing..." But what can you do? To
be all alone in the world, that's the worst... It's a job,
you know. You don't have to enjoy your job. Yo [△]

G

ROOM

'Tri Bywyd is performed at the site of a ruined farmhouse deep in a forest. It
weaves together the story of the ruined house itself and two other stories
from two other times and places in Wales - one a rural narrative, the other
an urban one. Three ghost houses are occupied by three ghost occupants,
who recount their tragic stories. From 1869, in Llanfihangel ar Arth near
Pencader,, the first house is Lletherneuadd Uchaf and its occupant is Sarah
Jacob, an eleven year old girl. From 1956, above Lampeter is Esgair Fraith - a
working hill farm. From 1988, in Butetown, Cardiff, the third house is 7 James
Street and its occupant is Linette White'

PO

XV

of the killing
seen right outside the
strange-looking man - obv
himself, mumbling, crying -
to hide his hand inside h
blood on it. It was evidenc
to 40 years of age and bc
photofit shows that stere
killer, with brown hair, wr
crimes in the world. Pub
Eventually, a psychologica
commissioned. And a susp

O S T / A N D / G H O S T / M A N

Brith Gof's Office

There was no concern for 'suitability' in bringing these three lives together.
Instead I wanted to avoid a kind of sensitive 'flower arranging' of themes. But
with hindsight it is clear that there are common elements to all three, and the
interweaving was a detailed but not impossible task. I was surprised how little
my choice of 'lives' was questioned - for it would have been difficult to justify

JAMES ST

7 JAMES STREET, BUTETOWN, CARDIFF - the flat where
Linette White was murdered - ordnance survey map

7 JAMES STREET, BUTETOWN, CARDIFF - the flat where
Linette White was murdered - aerial photograph

LOUISA PLACE

© Crown Copyright

LLETHERNEUADD UCHAF, LLANFIHANGEL AR ARTH, PENCADER, WALES
- the house where Sarah Jacob - The Welsh Fasting Girl - died.
Ordnance Survey Map

The Third Life is that of the young girl Sarah Jacob - who dies
on December 17th 1869, after a ten day vigil by nurses from
Guy's Hospital in London who were called in to determine
whether the child - known as The Welsh Fasting Girl - could,
as had been claimed, live without food or drink. Sarah occupies a site of great contention - between girl child and
woman, between Welsh rural 'backwardness' and English
urban 'sophistication', between religion and medical science.
Her 'project' is only made possible by the development of a
complete railway system linking all parts of Britain - allowing
her fame to spread across the land, and visitors to travel to
her parents' farmhouse - Lletherneuadd Uchaf - in the hills
above Pencader, to witness the miracle

5989

LLETHERNEUADD UCHAF, LLANFIHA
- the house where Sarah Jacob - Th
photograph

© Crown Copyright

3 4 5 6 7 8 9 10 11 5F

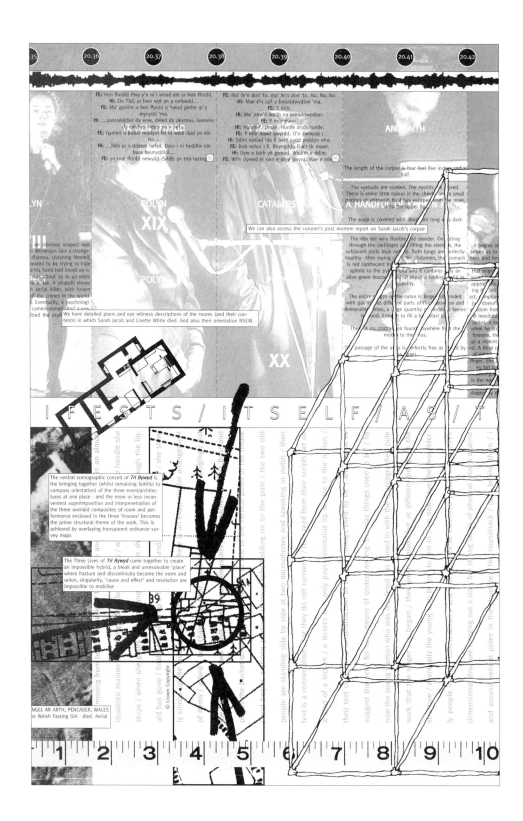

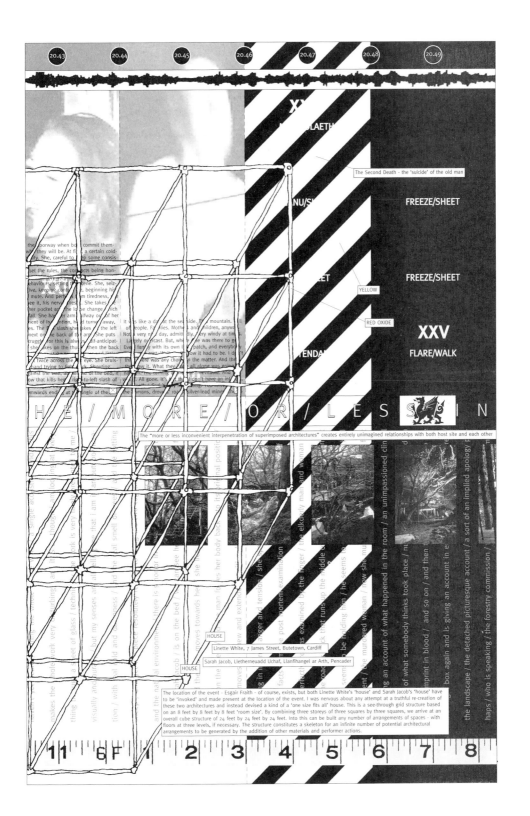

XX...

...LAETH

The Second Death - the 'suicide' of the old man

NU/S...

FREEZE/SHEET

...EET

FREEZE/SHEET

YELLOW

RED OXIDE

XXV
FLARE/WALK

...TENDA...

HE / MORE / OR / LES S IN

The "more or less inconvenient interpenetration of superimposed architectures" creates entirely unimagined relationships with both host site and each other

HOUSE

Linette White, 7 James Street, Butetown, Cardiff

Sarah Jacob, Lletherneuadd Uchaf, Llanfihangel ar Arth, Pencader

HOUSE

The location of the event - Esgair Fraith - of course, exists, but both Linette White's 'house' and Sarah Jacob's 'house' have to be 'invoked' and made present at the location of the event. I was nervous about any attempt at a truthful re-creation of these two architectures and instead devised a kind of a 'one size fits all' house. This is a see-through grid structure based on an 8 feet by 8 feet by 8 feet 'room size'. By combining three storeys of three squares by three squares, we arrive at an overall cube structure of 24 feet by 24 feet by 24 feet. Into this can be built any number of arrangements of spaces - with floors at three levels, if necessary. The structure constitutes a skeleton for an infinite number of potential architectural arrangements to be generated by the addition of other materials and performer actions.

11 6F 1 2 3 4 5 6 7 8

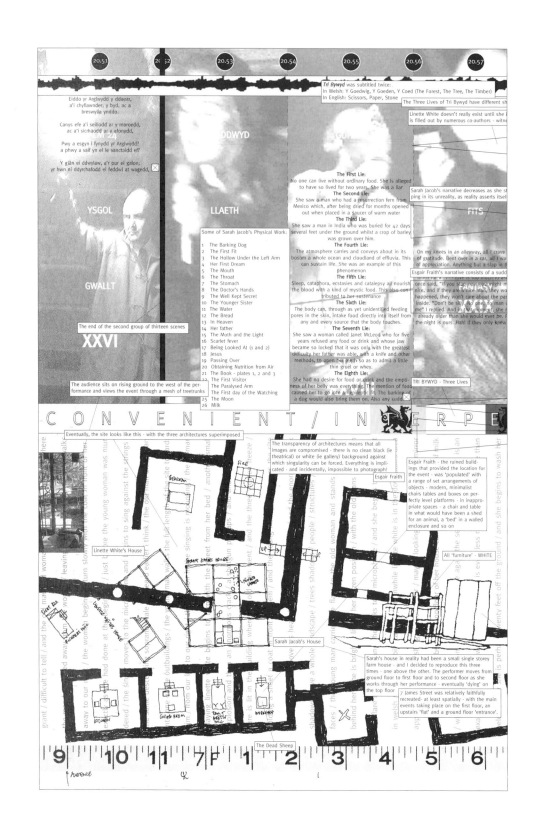

Eiddo yr Arglwydd y ddaear,
a'i chyflawnder; y byd, ac a
breswylia ynddo.

Canys efe a'i seiliodd ar y moroedd,
ac a'i sicodd ar y afonydd,

Pwy a esgyn i fynydd yr Arglwydd?
a phwy a saif yn ei le sanctaidd ef?

Y glân ei ddwylaw, a'r pur ei galon;
yr hwn ni ddyrchafodd ei feddwl at wagedd, ☒

YSGOL

GWALLT

XXVI

The end of the second group of thirteen scenes

The audience sits on rising ground to the west of the performance and views the event through a mesh of treetrunks

DDWYD

LLAETH

Tri Bywyd was subtitled twice:
In Welsh: Y Goedwig, Y Goeden, Y Coed (The Forest, The Tree, The Timber)
In English: Scissors, Paper, Stone

The Three Lives of Tri Bywyd have different sh

Linette White doesn't really exist until she
is filled out by numerous co-authors - witne

FITS

Some of Sarah Jacob's Physical Work:

1 The Barking Dog
2 The First Fit
3 The Hollow Under the Left Arm
4 Her First Dream
5 The Mouth
6 The Throat
7 The Stomach
8 The Doctor's Hands
9 The Well Kept Secret
10 The Younger Sister
11 The Water
12 The Bread
13 In Heaven
14 Her father
15 The Moth and the Light
16 Scarlet fever
17 Being Looked At (1 and 2)
18 Jesus
19 Passing Over
20 Obtaining Nutrition from Air
21 The Book - plates 1, 2 and 3
22 The First Visitor
23 The Paralysed Arm
24 The First day of The Watching
25 The Moon
26 Milk

The First Lie:
No one can live without ordinary food. She is alleged
to have so lived for two years. She was a liar
The Second Lie:
She saw a man who had a resurrection fern from
Mexico which, after being dried for months opened
out when placed in a saucer of warm water
The Third Lie:
She saw a man in India who was buried for 42 days
several feet under the ground whilst a crop of barley
was grown over him.
The Fourth Lie:
The atmosphere carries and conveys about in its
bosom a whole ocean and cloudland of effluvia. This
can sustain life. She was an example of this
phenomenon
The Fifth Lie:
Sleep, cataphora, ecstasies and catalepsy all nourish
the blood with a kind of mystic food. This also contributed to her sustenance
The Sixth Lie:
The body can, through as yet unidentified feeding
pores in the skin, intake food directly into itself from
any and every source that the body touches.
The Seventh Lie:
She saw a woman called Janet McLeod who for five
years refused any food or drink and whose jaw
became so locked that it was only with the greatest
difficulty her father was able, with a knife and other
methods, to open her teeth so as to admit a little
thin gruel or whey.
The Eighth Lie:
She had no desire for food or drink and the emptiness of her belly was everything. The mention of food
caused her to go into an epileptic fit. The barking of
a dog would also bring them on. Also any sudd ☒

On my knees in an alleyway, all I crave
of gratitude. Bent over in a car, all I wa
of appreciation. Anything but a slap in th

Esgair Fraith's narrative consists of a sudd
much for a ... - live is too much to as
once said, "If you stop now, you might m
nice, and if they are a nice man, they wo
happened, they won't care about the par
inside. "Don't be silly, No one, no man
me" I replied. And in that moment, I was
already older than she would ever be. F
the night is ours. Hah! If they only knew

TRI BYWYD - Three Lives

C O N V E N I E N T / I N   ERPE

Eventually, the site looks like this - with the three architectures superimposed

The transparency of architectures means that all
images are compromised - there is no clean black (ie
theatrical) or white (ie gallery) background against
which singularity can be forced. Everything is indicated - and incidentally, impossible to photograph!

Esgair Fraith - the ruined buildings that provided the location for
the event - was 'populated' with
a range of set arrangements of
objects - modern, minimalist
chairs tables and boxes on per-
fectly level platforms - in inappro-
priate spaces - a chair and table
in what would have been a shed
for an animal, a 'bed' in a walled
enclosure and so on

Esgair Fraith

Linette White's House

All 'furniture' - WHITE

Sarah Jacob's House

Sarah's house in reality had been a small single storey
farm house - and I decided to reproduce this three
times - one above the other. The performer moves from
ground floor to first floor and to second floor as she
works through her performance - eventually 'dying' on
the top floor

7 James Street was relatively faithfully
recreated - at least spatially - with the main
events taking place on the first floor, an
upstairs 'flat' and a ground floor 'entrance'.

The Dead Sheep

9   10   11   7F   1   2   3   4   5   6

The Third Death - Sarah Jacob starves to death

YELLOW

LLAD HEETS YNFAS FREEZE

Sarah Jacob's Ho

XXV

By the 6th Day - Thursday the 14th of December ... she
had had no food or drink and her appearance was
strained. Her voice was weaker as she read aloud.
Her pulse was 112. She had passed no urine since the
night before. By the afternoon her pulse ... it a new
smell abo ... the bed. She ... ... id ... pired hot
flannels to keep her warm.

... ... ay she stopped reading aloud. Her par-
... ... s to change her linen. She
... began to thro ... arms about

On ... ...orning of the 8th Day, it was ... to me ...
...ses that the child was not well. Sh ...
pin... nose, sunken eyes and an ar ...
abou ... face. Her mouth wa ... not once again ...
the pecu ... ... about her breath. Wh ...
... ...hat day he expressed alarm ...
... sought to ... suade her parent
... ...rink and f...

... ...become ... s...ffer...
... ...come de...us...
...younger ...ser wa...

TAS FREEZI

XXXVI

END FLARE/WALK

"It was
room. It
room ...
thing ...
to reas ...
English ...
... her t...
clean and
ness, that
you...

LAYERING / OF / ARCHIT

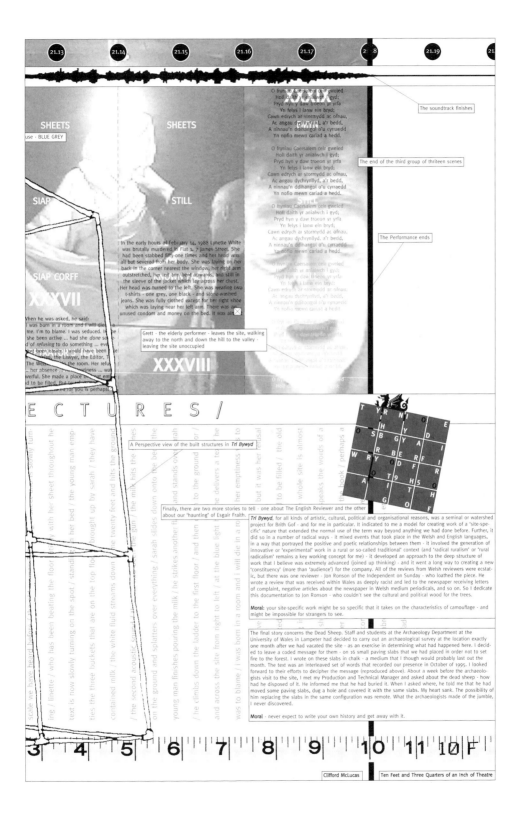

The soundtrack finishes

The end of the third group of thirteen scenes

The Performance ends

SHEETS

use · BLUE GREY

SHEETS

SIAP

STILL

SIAP CORFF

XXXVII

O fryniau Caersalem ceir gweled
Holl daith yr anialwch i gyd;
Pryd hyn y daw troeon yr yrfa
Yn felys i lanw ein bryd;
Cawn edrych ar stormydd ac ofnau,
Ac angau dychrynllyd, a'r bedd,
A ninnau'n ddihangol o'u cyrraedd
Yn nofio mewn cariad a hedd.

O fryniau Caersalem ceir gweled
Holl daith yr anialwch i gyd;
Pryd hyn y daw troeon yr yrfa
Yn felys i lanw ein bryd;
Cawn edrych ar stormydd ac ofnau,
Ac angau dychrynllyd, a'r bedd,
A ninnau'n ddihangol o'u cyrraedd
Yn nofio mewn cariad a hedd.

O fryniau Caersalem ceir gweled
Holl daith yr anialwch i gyd;
Pryd hyn y daw troeon yr yrfa
Yn felys i lanw ein bryd;
Cawn edrych ar stormydd ac ofnau,
Ac angau dychrynllyd, a'r bedd,
A ninnau'n ddihangol o'u cyrraedd
Yn nofio mewn cariad a hedd.

In the early hours of February 14, 1988 Lynette White was brutally murdered in Flat 1, 7 James Street. She had been stabbed fifty-one times and her head was all but severed from her body. She was laying on her back in the corner nearest the window, her right arm outstretched, her left arm bent upwards, and still in the sleeve of the jacket which lay across her chest. Her head was turned to the left. She was wearing two t-shirts – one grey, one black – and stone-washed jeans. She was fully clothed except for her right shoe which was laying near her left arm. There was an unused condom and money on the bed. It was ai[...]

When he was asked, he said:
I was born in a room and I will die ... me. I'm to blame. I was seduced. In ... she been active ... had she done so ... d of refusing to do something ... eve ... had been easier. I would have been ... Wife?, the Lawyer, the Editor, T ... The Watch... in the room. Her refu ... her absence ... ... was ... werful. She made a place ... at em... d to be filled. But ... ... for you is perhaps ...

Grett - the elderly performer - leaves the site, walking away to the north and down the hill to the valley · leaving the site unoccupied

XXXVIII

ECTURES /

A Perspective view of the built structures in *Tri Bywyd*

scale we have heard / ing / linette / who has been beating the floor ... with her sheet throughout he / text is now slowly turning on the spot / standing in her bed / the young man emp- / ties the three buckets that are on the top floor, brought up by sarah / they have / contained milk / the white fluid streams down the twenty feet and hits the ground / the second acoustic ... / on the ground and splatters over everything / sarah slides down onto the be... / young man finishes pouring the milk / he strikes another ... / he delivers a fe... / he climbs down the ladder to the first floor / and then ... / and across the site from right to left / at the blue light ... / was to blame / i was born in a room and i will die in a ro...

Finally, there are two more stories to tell · one about The English Reviewer and the other about our 'haunting' of Esgair Fraith.

Tri Bywyd, for all kinds of artistic, cultural, political and organisational reasons, was a seminal or watershed project for Brith Gof - and for me in particular. It indicated to me a model for creating work of a 'site-specific' nature that extended the normal use of the term way beyond anything we had done before. Further, it did so in a number of radical ways · it mixed events that took place in the Welsh and English languages, in a way that portrayed the positive and poetic relationships between them · it involved the generation of innovative or 'experimental' work in a rural or so-called traditional context (and 'radical ruralism' or 'rural radicalism' remains a key working concept for me) · it developed an approach to the deep structure of work that I believe was extremely advanced (joined up thinking) · and it went a long way to creating a new 'constituency' (more than 'audience') for the company. All of the reviews from Welsh reviewers were ecstatic, but there was one reviewer · Jon Ronson of the Independent on Sunday · who loathed the piece. He wrote a review that was racist within Wales as deeply racist and led to the newspaper receiving letters of complaint, negative articles about the newspaper in Welsh medium periodicals, and so on. So I dedicate this documentation to Jon Ronson · who couldn't see the cultural and political wood for the trees.

Moral: your site-specific work might be so specific that it takes on the characteristics of camouflage - and might be impossible for strangers to see.

The final story concerns the Dead Sheep. Staff and students at the Archaeology Department at the University of Wales in Lampeter had decided to carry out an archaeological survey at the location exactly one month after we had vacated the site - as an exercise in determining what had happened here. I decided to leave a coded message for them - on 16 small paving slabs that we had placed in order not to set fire to the forest. I wrote on these slabs in chalk - a medium that I though would probably last out the month. The text was an interleaved set of words that recorded our presence in October of 1995. I looked forward to their efforts to decipher the message (reproduced above). About a week before the archaeologists visit to the site, I met my Production and Technical Manager and asked about the dead sheep - how had he disposed of it. He informed me that he had buried it. When I asked where, he told me that he had moved some paving slabs, dug a hole and covered it with the same slabs. My heart sank. The possibility of him replacing the slabs in the same configuration was remote. What the archaeologists made of the jumble, I never discovered.

Moral - never expect to write your own history and get away with it.

3   4   5   6   7   8   9   10   11   10 F

Clifford McLucas | Ten Feet and Three Quarters of an Inch of Theatre

Materials

Just as there is a logic of words or of drawings, there is a logic of materials, and these are not the same. And, however much they are subverted, something ultimately resists [. . .] A word is not a concrete block.

(Tschumi 1994d: 252)

Where mapping elaborates the complexity of *knowing* the site, the address to a 'logic of materials' which emerged in European sculpture and North American post-minimal art from the late 1960s tested the most conventional of distinctions between the work and its physical location. In identifying the 'logic of materials' with processes of transformation, in deploying materials as catalysts for change, or defining the artwork as a point of intersection between processes, these practices frequently aligned the nature and affect of materials with notions of event and performance, challenging the material integrity of the object and the stability of place and location. Here, not only is site-specificity defined in exchanges between visual art and performance, and between materials and events, but, in the wake of minimalism and land art, the body also became a key aspect of the terms through which the site and the site-specific work were elaborated.

Material Affects: Gilberto Zorio, Giovanni Anselmo, Giuseppe Penone

In his influential article 'Anti-Form' of 1968, Robert Morris addressed the relationship between form and materials characterising the 'so-called Minimal or Object art' (Morris 1993b: 41). Associating the geometrical forms of this 'object-type art' with an exposure of the rigid materials of which it is constructed, Morris argued that never before had 'the cubic and the rectangular been brought so far forward into the final definition of the work' (Morris 1993b: 41). Yet here Morris also describes a potentially debilitating circumscription of means. Arguing that in minimalist construction a 'morphology of geometric, predominantly rectangular forms has been accepted as a given premise' (Morris 1993b: 41), Morris observes that the very methods which had fostered this visibility of materials had by 1968 become narrowly prescriptive, that in this work 'it is the *a priori* valuation of the well built that dictates the materials. The well-built form of objects preceded any consideration of means. Materials themselves have been limited to those that efficiently make the general object form' (Morris 1993b: 45–6).

In the 'systemic' forms deployed by artists such as Sol LeWitt, Donald Judd and Carl Andre, in which multiple units rather than single unitary forms were deployed in repetitive or progressive arrangements, Morris argues, this formal logic becomes explicit, as the very 'rationality' of these ordering systems is 'related to the reasonableness of the well built' (Morris 1993b: 41–3). Where such 'reasonableness' prevails, he concludes, an opposition between given 'materials' and the principle by which they are ordered becomes explicit, and the abstract order supersedes the architectonic and material properties of any of these individual units, for

> any order for multiple units is an imposed one that has no
> inherent relation to the physicality of the existing units.
> Permuted, progressive, symmetrical organisations have a dualistic
> character in relation to the matter they distribute. This is not to
> imply that these simple orderings do not work. They simply
> separate, more or less, from what is physical by making
> relationships themselves another order of facts [. . .] The duality
> is established by the fact that an order, any order, is operating
> beyond the physical things.
>
> (Morris 1993b: 41–3)

In response Morris considers an emphasis upon 'the process of "making itself"' (Morris 1993b: 43), recalling Jackson Pollock's use of a 'drip' technique in creating his action paintings where, he argues, in acknowledging 'the inherent tendencies and properties' of his materials Pollock was able 'to recover process and hold onto it as part of the end form of the work' (Morris 1993b: 43). In recent sculpture by Eva Hess, Richard Serra and Barry Le Va, Morris observes, where 'materials other than rigid industrial ones have begun to show up' (Morris 1993b: 46), analogous concerns with process have resurfaced.

Indeed, by 1968 concerns with the 'tendencies and properties' of matter were apparent not only in the work of New York-based artists, including Morris himself, but in a new wave of European sculpture associated with the *arte povera* movement burgeoning around Turin, Milan and Rome. Defined by the critic Germano Celant following the exhibition *Arte povera* at the La Bertesca Gallery in Genoa in 1967 and, one month later, in the international art-journal *Flash Art*'s publication of Celant's manifesto 'Arte povera: appunti per una guerriglia' ('Arte povera: notes for a guerrilla war') (Celant 1967), *arte povera* had its immediate roots in the work and influence of Michelangelo Pistoletto, Piero Gilardi, and Mario Merz in Turin, Jannis Kounellis in Rome, and a new generation of northern Italian artists who began exhibiting work under their influence in 1966 and 1967, including Gilberto Zorio, Giovanni Anselmo, Giuseppe Penone, Alighiero Boetti, and Luciano Fabro. Yet, while defining the emergence of *arte povera* around these artists' work, Celant also associated the movement with a wide range of activities, including many of those described by Morris. Celant's 1969 volume cataloguing *Arte Povera: Conceptual, Actual or Impossible Art?* (Celant 1969) included Morris' large felt pieces, work by North American artists such as Carl Andre, Douglas Heubler, Dennis Oppenheim, Michael Heizer, Eva Hesse, Richard Serra, and the English artist Richard Long, alongside Pistoletto, Merz, Penone, Zorio, Boetti, Fabro as well as the German artist Hans Haacke and the collaborative performance group, *Lo Zoo*, founded by Pistoletto. This account of *arte povera* touches not only upon sculpture, installation and notions

of 'anti-form', but land art, conceptual art and performance, drawing
on an eclectic range of post-minimal and process-based activities which,
in various ways, erode or break down the constraints of the object form
Morris describes. For Celant, Carolyn Christov-Bakargiev argues in her
detailed assessment of early *arte povera* work, this 'moment of aesthetic
rebellion' meant

> freedom from an alienating rationalistic system, from coherence,
> from optical art, Pop art and minimalism. [Celant] speaks of a
> 'poor' art as opposed to a complex one, of an art that does not
> add ideas or things to the world but that discovers what's already
> there.
>
> (Christov-Bakargiev 1987: 53)

In this context, the early work of artists such as Zorio, Anselmo and
Penone directly challenged the conventional opposition between 'physical things' and the 'abstract order' of the artwork, opening the sculpture
to forces and events precipitated by the presence of materials, to
'natural' or organic processes identified with particular locations as well
as to exchanges between material processes, the environment and the
body. As this implies, in foregrounding the properties of 'matter', such
work tends toward a 'dedifferentiation' (Morris 1993: 61) between the
materials and forms of art and, subsequently, between the work and its
environment. Here, too, the relationship between the object and its
context reaches, through sculpture, toward performance.

Emphasising his attraction to 'all processes of "suspension," where
one can find the roots of an action or a moment' (Celant 1991: 55),
Gilberto Zorio presents materials and objects which, in implying or
precipitating events, assert a relationship with their material, spatial or
environmental contexts. In early presentations such as *Rosa – Blu – Rosa*
(*Pink – Blue – Pink*) (1967), consisting of an eternit semi-cylinder of
cobalt chloride whose reaction to changes of humidity in the room in
which it is placed cause gradual changes in its colour, or *Piombi* (*Lead*)
(1968), whose combination of lead, copper, water and hydrochloric acid

produces the slow event of electrolysis, Zorio staged objects whose characteristics are defined through ongoing processes. Citing Zorio's 'interest in energy transformations, in the tensions and passages between one material and another' (Celant 1991: 29), Germano Celant reads such phenomena as '"living" work in which the representation of visual phenomena cannot be distinguished from the physical process the substances undergo' (Celant 1991: 33). Here, the order of 'physical things' includes *events* and *processes*. In this context, Zorio has also played on the semantic function of the object, where the work at once signals and threatens to precipitate a specific event. In revisiting a series of 'excessive signs of energy' (Amann 1976) including the five-pointed star, the alchemical crucible, and the javelin, by deploying lasers or live electrical circuits, and by incorporating agents of radical change including acid, heat, and even fire into his presentations, Zorio has placed 'precarious, excessive signs' (Celant 1991: 67) into situations where the sculpture threatens a collapse under the release of the very forces it signifies. *Stella incandescente* (*Incandescent Star*) (1973), for example, presents a situation incorporating risk in the form of a suspended incandescent electrical circuit in the shape of the five-pointed star, contact with which may kill. *Stella di giavellotti* (*Star of Javelins*) (1974) forms the same star from javelins locked together in a state of extreme tension, creating, Werner Lippert suggests, 'a real energy system' (Lippert 1976). In these pieces, the potential of radical and sudden change, of intrusion and collapse, is explicitly a part of the material properties of the work. Thus, *Stella di giavelotti* offers, Ugo Castagnotto suggests, not simply the 'image of energy but the energy of an image' for '[s]eizing the javelins unmakes the star and, at the same time, reveals its energy content' (Castagnotto 1976).

In these imbrications of the object with potential or actual events, Zorio explicitly works against the conventional containment of the sculptural work. Indeed, here, the conceptual order and stability implied by the object form becomes a ground *against which* events or occurrences which elude or are in excess of this order are defined. Always working, in this sense, towards an excess, these installations are constituted in multiple processes and relationships, and so defined, Denys Zacharopolous suggests, as 'a point of intersection of several fields of action in the world' where '[w]hat bothers the order of things is that there is not just a single order' (Zacharopolous 1996: 190).

This excessive aspect of Zorio's presentations, where a work is revealed in an interplay of processes or systems, has led directly to performance in a privileging of event over object. For *Microfoni* (*Microphones*) (1968–69), an installation related to the series *Per purificare le parole* (*For the Purification of Words*), Zorio set a series of microphones and speakers around a single gallery room, creating a system which amplified, echoed and so multiplied specific, performed utterances by its visitors while also picking up background or unintended sounds and conversation. Designed to release the plastic properties of words, *Microfoni* transforms the spoken utterance into an abstract, seemingly malleable, and so 'sculptural', material. In relation to this piece, Zorio observes that '[a] word absorbed by a microphone and repeated over and over by a loudspeaker loses its literal significance and becomes a sound, incomprehensible but mentally and physically perceptible' (Celant 1991).

Exemplifying Zorio's notion of a 'plastic event' (Zorio 1996), *Microfoni* releases the potential of words and sounds to acquire the formal properties of an abstract material, properties *in excess* of their semantic function. In doing so, this installation challenges the opposition between the artwork and its immediate circumstances, and collapses the 'abstract order' of a work into the very tendencies and properties of ambient and performed sounds. Yet *Microfoni* also invokes the object as a foil to the event. In releasing the plastic, sculptural aspect of performed utterances, *Microfoni* looks toward a *shaping* of this material. In operating at 'a point of intersection of several fields of action' (Zacharopolous 1996: 190), however, this work will be continually reconstituted in the site's arbitrary events and circumstances, and so realised as an order which is always *in performance*. *Microfoni*, finally, is formed in these tensions, where the circumstances of the site are inseparable from the material and form of the sculptural work, and where, in order to be realised, the 'object' must be performed. Consistently with this, Zorio emphasises that his interest in this piece is not in any possible resolution, but in 'this very effort to show itself', in 'a continuous revelation of energy' (Celant 1991: 47). It is in this tension, too, that *Microfoni*'s site-specificity is defined, where the materials of the site continually redefine the work, but the work ensures that all occurrences are subject to its processes. Thus, Zorio emphasises, '[i]t was important for me to achieve an "enveloping" space ready to assimilate all things and events. And if the spectator did not like the things and events he produced, he produced them anyway' (Celant 1991: 39).

Just as the unfolding of this 'plastic event' calls into question the opposition between the work and the site, so *Microfoni* identifies the viewer's presence with the material and medium of the work. Where *Rosa – Blu – Rosa* responded to the viewer's bodily presence in *chemical* terms, this installation engenders and realises the visitor's performance, rendering her activity indistinguishable from the *materials* of a site-specific work. In this respect, *Microfoni* also reflects another aspect of this tension between object and event, which Zorio proposes as the 'concept of transition or identification between body and sculpture' (Celant 1991: 43). Indeed, this is a concept to which these concerns with the properties and tendencies of materials continually return.

Giovanni Anselmo's installations extend this address to the relationship between the material properties of the work and its location. Anselmo's first pieces, of 1965 and 1966, purposefully questioned the boundaries between sculptural material and environmental phenomena. *Senza titolo* (*untitled*) (1965) and *Senza titolo* (*untitled*) (1966), which articulate tensions between weight and suspension, are catalogued by Anselmo as incorporating iron, wood and 'force of gravity' (Anselmo 1989: 161). It is a vocabulary which reflects Anselmo's concern to reveal the relationships at play in and on the material's occupation of site and space. Indeed, rather than conceive of the sculptural work as resolved into a *form*, Anselmo proposes that his installations are, in effect, 'the physication [*sic*] of the force of an action, of the energy of a situation or event, etc.' (Celant 1969: 109). Thus, in reference to *Torsione* (*Torsion*)

(1968), in which a heavy iron bar is installed against a wall in a state of extreme torsion, Anselmo concludes that '[i]t is necessary [. . .] that the energy of a torsion lives with its true force; it certainly wouldn't live just by its form' (Celant 1969: 109).

This exposure of forces has immediate consequences for the reading of the border or limits of Anselmo's work. In placing objects in situations of extreme torsion or heavy pieces of stone into temporary suspension (*Senza titolo* [*untitled*] 1980, *Senza titolo* [*untitled*] 1984–6), Anselmo *works against* the object's isolation. Indeed, these objects and materials are deployed in order to articulate and intervene into a latent balance between forces, and to provoke a potential *disequilibrium* and physical exchange. It is in this disequilibrium, which reveals these materials' definition of and in the site, that Anselmo's works articulate their specificity to site. Anselmo stresses that '[m]y objects are physical energy, the forces are channelled and directed to a point so that, in the various works, you have an unstable equilibrium, potential motion, tension, and compression' (Ponti 1996: 79). Here, where, as Anselmo observes, '[t]he structure of these situations and the visual elements of my objects are subordinated' (Ponti 1996: 79), the very idea that the artwork can be located *as an object* is challenged. For the German artist Hans Haacke, this exposure of an intimate exchange between the material of sculpture and the forces and processes of its environment overthrows precisely the containment implied by the object form. In relation to his own early work, such as *Live Airborne System* (1964), encompassing birds feeding at sea, or *Grass Grows* (1967), a conic pile of earth which is gradually covered by grass, Haacke developed a concept of sculpture as 'real-time systems' in exchange with environmental processes. Here, Haacke concludes,

A 'sculpture' that physically reacts to its environment and/or affects its surroundings is no longer to be regarded as an object. The range of outside factors influencing it, as well as its own radius of action, reach beyond the space it materially occupies. It thus merges with the environment in a relationship that is

better understood as a 'system' of interdependent processes [. . .]
A system is not imagined; it is real.

(Celant 1969: 179)

This interaction of systems has direct implications for the viewer.
Where the sculptural work operates *in* and *through* the systems and
materials of 'its' environment, so the viewer's maintenance of a position *outside* the work becomes untenable. *Rosa – Blu – Rosa* responds
not simply to ambient humidity, but to the material affect of the body,
and so to the body as a 'real-time system'. Here, the viewer finds herself
in the site-specific work, as a participant in a chemical interaction
defining a specific sculptural process. For Zorio, this interaction reflects
a direct equation between the object and the body, derived, he suggests,
from an 'inner vision of the body' which 'comes to me [. . .] from
viewing it in chemical terms', where '[e]ach human is a container of
minerals and water; his veins, lungs and organs are an extraordinary
chemistry lab made of tubes and alembics' (Celant 1991: 37). *Rosa –
Blu – Rosa* in particular, Werner Lippert argues, offers itself precisely
according to Haacke's formulation, where:

> As a real-time system, this work reacts proportionally to the
> variations in the system in which it is set (gallery-volume
> environment, humidity of the air) [. . .] it reacts to anyone who
> uses it; that is, to anyone whose presence varies the system, the
> presence being necessary for perception.

(Lippert 1976)

For Anselmo, where the placement of materials works against the
attempt to read the bounded interior of a work, so it also works to
disturb the viewer's sense of her body's *differentiation* or isolation from
the materials she confronts, and so its physical and spatial integrity.
Indeed, in revealing an intimate exchange between 'materials' and
'environment', these installations implicate the viewer's own presence
into their material terms, provoking a sense of participation *in* the site,

and so of a phenomenological exchange. In an interview of 1997, and reflecting upon his work's articulation of active forces and relationships, Anselmo emphasised that

> a successful piece of art is like a meeting point where energies go
> and from which energies depart. It's a moment of tension
> between the inside and the outside, in all senses: in the personal
> sense and in the sense of the space. [. . .] From my point of view,
> I'm putting in relationship my inside with this story outside.
>
> (Anselmo 1996)

In placing 'interventions in nature against the limitations of his own body' (Amann 1977: 74), Giuseppe Penone's work has elaborated and tested this affinity between body, object and environment. Articulating relationships between geological, organic, biological and sculptural processes, where a 'dedifferentiation' between organic and inorganic processes becomes explicit, Penone's work asserts equivalencies between conventionally distinct materials and material processes. Thus, he proposes, 'there is human material and there are materials called stone and wood, which together make up cities, railroads, and streets, riverbeds and mountains' (Celant 1989: 19). It is a relationship which Penone expresses in analogies and exchanges between body, work and environment, and so, he argues, through 'a relationship between the breathing of one material with respect to the other. In my opinion the elements are fluid, even stone is fluid, a mountain crumbles and becomes sand, it's just a matter of time' (Celant 1989: 17). In this context, however, Penone's work is shaped by an anthropological or anthropomorphic imperative. He argues that:

> It is difficult to understand the work of the human being if this
> work is integrated into nature: if I make a stone exactly like a
> river stone, nobody notices the difference. If instead I make a
> head, it becomes significant. There is a human incapacity to
> understand something that is just not like us.
>
> (Celant 1989: 21)

Indeed, in confronting organic or inorganic material with the body, Penone acts out a specific reversal. Rather than treat the body as a material or 'real-time system', Penone treats materials as the body, so realising an 'anthropological' aspect implicit within both Zorio and Anselmo's approach to materials and site. Zorio recognises precisely this equivalence and exchange in his own work, where, he emphasises, not only does the presence of the javelin recall the human hand or the body (Celant 1991: 53), but his focus upon energy itself 'is neither an abstract note nor something purely physical, but it implies a total human dimension, an anthropological dimension' (Amann 1976).

Penone's early work addressing 'the real time of growth' (Celant 1989: 55) crystallises this exchange. In *Alpi Marittime* (*Maritime Alps*) (1968–1978), *Senza titolo* (*untitled*) (1973) and *I colori dei temporali* (*The Colours of Storms*) (1987), Penone intervened into the process of a tree's growth, penetrating the tree with a sculpted model of his hand, or altering its course by imposing weights or affixing a bronze branch to the trunk. In these interventions into a tree's definition of its form in growth in its natural environment, Penone pursues exchanges between materials and processes which set their own equilibrium over extended periods of time. Here, Penone suggests,

> I was imagining a different density of matter: wood, a hard material, becomes fluid and soft with time. I explored the relationship between the life-time, the breath of the tree and my breath, seen as natural but opposite elements [. . .] it has many phases of development, and every moment can be final.
>
> (Celant 1989: 17)

Here, the *form* of the work arises out of the response of organic processes to a specific intervention. Indeed, here, the tree acts out a living process which Penone's intervention invests with an anthropomorphism, as the tree's growth is articulated in relation to the properties and faculties of a sentient viewer. For his documentation of *I colori dei temporali*, Penone reflected on this process, where 'The tree, as it builds vertically, continuously searches for equilibrium and carries out, in the number of its branches and the weight and distribution of its leaves, the same analysis of the void as the tightrope-walker with his outstretched arms' (Celant 1989: 45).

Fundamentally, here, as with Zorio and Anselmo, there is no solid or stable ground to be established as *the site*. Indeed, here, materials are never static. Site, under this logic, *is* a complex of chemical, organic, physiological and biological systems, interacting and affecting one another, and so a complex of relations always *in process*. Furthermore, this is a logic which, for Penone, provides for relationships between materials, material processes and sculpture. The tree, he suggests,

> is memory, it traverses [. . .] as it grows and records its form in its structure. The tree is fluid, clay is fluid, stone is fluid, water is fluid. Fluids conserve memory, fluids are memory. All materials preserve the memory of their experience, in their form. The ability to recognise and decipher memory is culture. The memory of a contact, of an action, is culture. Sculpture is the revelation of the form of memory.
>
> (Penone 1989: 184)

In this sculpture, the operation of an abstract order which supersedes the properties of materials, and which Morris identified with late-minimalism, is resolved and inverted. Indeed, Penone argues, this sculpture's purpose is, finally, 'to find the form within the material, not to use the material to find the form' (Penone 1996). In this focus upon material properties, the site-specific work occurs as *interventions* into unfolding complexes of inter-related biological, organic and inorganic processes, which have implications for the material, space, time and 'body' of the work. Here, the 'anthropological dimension' of site-specific sculpture is realised not simply in *forms*, but in *the performance of the site itself*: in interventions into the energy, actions and processes which materials precipitate and in those processes and exchanges which express material affinities between the body, the object and the environment it defines and is defined by. In this process-based work, Penone suggests, 'every moment can be final', and yet each moment, and material form, retains a memory and trace of the process of which it is a part.

Embodying Site: Dennis Oppenheim and Vito Acconci

Where Penone's work has emphasised the 'anthropological dimension' (Amann 1976) of materials and material processes, Dennis Oppenheim and Vito Acconci's entry into body art in New York in the late 1960s transposed the prevailing logic and terms of sculpture and sculptural process on to the body. Here, under the influence of land art and minimalism, these artists addressed the work's relationship to its site through a construction of the performing body itself as means, material and *place*.

Oppenheim's entry into performance was shaped in his critical address to the studio ideology of the gallery. Here, by presenting objects as residue or a trace of sites and activities *elsewhere*, Oppenheim worked to displace the centrality of both the gallery and the object. In his first exhibited works, *Sitemarkers*, of 1967, Oppenheim designated a series of specific sites around New York (Heiss 1992: 8), showing a photographic image, a record of each location, and an aluminium marker engraved with the site's number. *One Hour Run* of 1968 extended this attempt to counter the assumption that the artwork should be 'isolated from everything that would detract from its evaluation of itself' (O'Docherty 1986: 14). Here Oppenheim 'parodied action painting by cutting snowmobile tracks intuitively or expressively in the snow for one hour' (McEvilley 1992: 20), so inscribing a signature mark of Modernist painting over a specific locality in an attack upon the art object's autonomy. 'For me,' Oppenheim argued in a key interview with the critic Willoughby Sharp of 1971, 'activity on land is *charged*, not passive like processed steel. Land holds traces of a dynamic past, which the artist may allow to enter his work if he so wishes' (Sharp 1971:

188). However, it is finally the photographic image of *One Hour Run*, as documentation, which works against this Modernist abstraction, in a form which is not only lent the *mark* of abstract expressionism, but, in the gallery, its pictorial field, its availability and even its '*sellability*' (Kaye 1996: 66).

It is in this context that Oppenheim's sculptural practices define his entry into performance. Thus, in an effort to counter the work's resolution into the art object, *Sound Enclosed Land Area* of the early summer of 1969 introduced an exchange between body and site in the form of 'a sound tape of my footsteps while I walked around a selected area

Dennis Oppenheim: *One Hour Run*, 1968. 6-mile continuous track cut with a 10 h.p. snowmobile repeating the continuous route for an hour, 1′ × 3′ × 6 miles. St Francis, Maine, U.S.A. Courtesy of Dennis Oppenheim.

of the city' (Sharp 1971: 186). For Oppenheim this process 'implied a re-acceptance of the manual, physical aspect of art-making' (Sharp 1971: 186), yet it also positioned the body at the centre of a process of documentation. Played in the gallery, this record of Oppenheim's physical activity is positioned as a map and memory of a particular place, and the trace of one site is mediated into another. It is a tactic which Oppenheim elaborated in his subsequent address to the material properties of the gallery building. In *Weight Displacement* for the 'Art by Telephone' show in Chicago in 1969, Oppenheim proposed using his 'changing physical condition as a measure of control' (Sharp 1971:

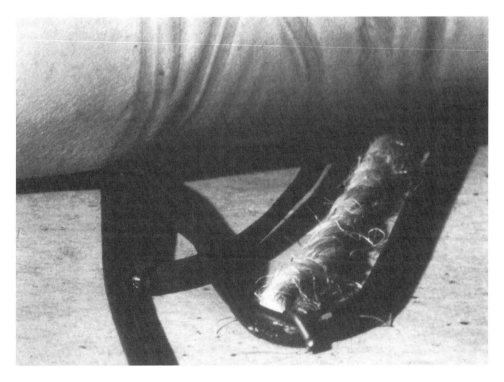

Dennis Oppenheim: *Arm and Wire*, 1969, with Bob Fiore. 8min 16mm silent Sept. Here the arm is receiving impressions of its own energy. Material vs. tool loses distinction as the results of an action are fed back to the source. Courtesy of Dennis Oppenheim.

186) for a piece in which the constituent elements of the gallery room would act as a measure and memory of his body. Here, Oppenheim recounts:

> I asked that piles of five materials prominent in the construction of the museum be distributed on the museum floor in piles equal to my weight at the time of the installation [. . .] Each week the museum would call me and adjust the piles according to my weight. My everyday activities were thus controlling the proportions of the material.
>
> (Sharp 1971: 186)

In 1970, this series of exchanges between the body and a specific site culminated in the execution of a live performance as a measure of a specific terrain. For *Two Jumps for Dead Dog Creek*, Oppenheim attempted a series of standing jumps at a selected site in Idaho, where '[t]he width of the creek became a specific goal to which I geared a bodily activity' (Sharp 1971: 188). His two successful jumps, he argued, defined a 'specific energy distribution' which had been 'dictated by a land form' (Sharp 1971: 188). Here, in performing a mapping of one place through another, Oppenheim comes to resolve a sculptural process in a live event. Thus, in the repetition of this activity at the John Gibson Gallery in New York in May 1970, Thomas McEvilley argues, 'the artist's body became the mediating device that brought outside and inside together' (McEvilley 1992: 21). In executing this act, Oppenheim concluded, '[f]or a split second, a physical tolerance was fused with an exterior location. I did the jump twice and succeeded both times. That place was now *embodied*' (Sharp 1971: 188–9).

Where Oppenheim sought to *embody* place, Acconci's entry into performance in 1969, prompted by his concern for '"real space time" [. . .] "actual space time"' (Acconci 1978), focused upon the relationships between the art object, its site, and the viewer. In these respects, and like a wide range of body art performance, Acconci's work responded to the latent anthropomorphism and 'theatricality' of the minimal object (Fried 1968: 142). Indeed, Robert Morris had himself recognised the 'anthropological' aspects of the unitary form, which, he suggested in 'Notes on Sculpture, Part Four: Beyond Objects',

> shares the perceptual response we have toward figures. This is undoubtedly why subliminal, generalised kinaesthetic responses are strong in confronting object art. Such responses are often denied or repressed because they seem so patently inappropriate in the face of nonanthropological forms, yet they are there. Even in subtle morphological ways, object-type art is tied to the body.
>
> (Morris 1993: 54)

For Acconci, minimalism's confrontation with the body, its demand that one must recognise 'the fact that art obviously had to be this relation between whatever it was that started off the art and the viewer' (Acconci 1982), implied an engagement with the performative transactions underpinning both the site and the conventional limits of the artwork. Thus, in *Performance Test* of 1969, Acconci occupied the stage of a small theatre, 'sitting on a chair, centre stage, facing the audience: staring at each of them in turn, from left to right, front to back, for thirty seconds each' (Acconci 1972: 45). Here, in performing minimalism's reversal of the viewer's gaze, Acconci forces an incursion of unpredictable, uncomfortable and private exchanges into the 'condition of reception' (Crimp 1993: 16) defining its site-specificity. Faced with this confrontation, Acconci recalls, the piece unfolds through a series of exchanges, where:

> Audience looks at performance, performance looks back at it –
> the gaze of the audience [. . .] is turned back on itself. Performer
> stares: viewer stares back. Performer stares: viewer starts to stare,
> can't hold the stare, drops off, the viewer gets through. Viewer is
> already staring when the performer reaches him: performer has
> to entwine his stare around the viewer's. Viewer refuses to stare,
> then looks up to check if performer is still staring: viewer caught

by performer. Performer stares: viewer refuses to stare back,
keeps looking away: performer's stare loses its point, becomes
dispersed.

(Acconci 1972: 45)

Where minimalism blurred the boundaries of the work in the evacuated, 'aesthetic' space of the 'White-Cube' gallery, *Performance Test* acts
out an intrusion into the private, peripheral space of audience activity.
Rather than deflect attention back toward the viewer's physical occupation of the gallery space, Acconci's stare demands that the viewer
perform the limits of the *public* work by responding to his insistent
intrusion into her ostensibly *private* realm. In extending this address to
the social as well as aesthetic boundaries of the work, Acconci also
worked to infringe one site with the terms of another. In *Service Area*,
shown as part of the 'Information' show at the Museum of Modern
Art, New York, in the summer of 1970, Acconci had his personal mail
forwarded to the museum, 'transforming the exhibition space into a
mailbox and annexing the postal service to art' (Linker 1994: 20). For
Room Piece of January 1970, Acconci proposed that:

> Each weekend the contents of one room of my apartment
> (Christopher St) are relocated at Gain Ground Gallery (West
> 80th St) [. . .] The items relocated at Gain Ground are used as
> they would ordinarily be used inside my apartment. Whenever I
> need something that has been relocated at Gain Ground, I go
> there to get it; anything taken out of the gallery is returned when
> I have finished using it.

(Acconci 1972: 16)

Here, Acconci disperses the work *outward* toward events in excess of
the frameworks and functions of the gallery. Analogously to Oppenheim's performed documentation of a specific site, this evidencing of
another place effects an incursion of seemingly peripheral, ostensibly
'non-art', behaviours and purposes into the artwork. For Oppenheim,

it is precisely this sense of a deferral toward the object's *periphery*, which prompts an incursion into a 'dematerialized zone' (Kaye 1996: 66) of performance. In this mode of work, Oppenheim stresses,

> *in spirit*, there was the feeling that these activities were charges to activate the periphery of things. There was a tendency to see even discrete performances and works as being charges that opened up doors that were not going to be found on the paper that you were presenting the work to.
>
> (Kaye 1996: 63)

However, for both Acconci and Oppenheim, this pressing toward contents operating at the limit of the conventional artwork is carried forward most effectively in actions approaching or embodying place.

In *Two Jumps for Dead Dog Creek* Oppenheim's performance presents itself not only *in relation* to a specific site but *in its place*: here, in fact, not only is the body engaged in a mapping of the site, but this performance of the dimensions of a specific place maps out the physical tolerances of the body. Indeed, by 1970, Oppenheim had filmed a series of actions equating activities on the body and on land. In actions such as *Arm and Asphalt* (1969), Oppenheim suggests, 'I was interested in land as a parallel surface to skin' (Sharp 1971: 187). Here, in acting out a direct physical exchange with a site or material in which his body is scarred or marked, Oppenheim would 'correlate a specific body surface to an exterior location. When my body met the land, the scar which was formed became a permanent record of the transaction' (*sic*) (Sharp 1971: 187–88). In *Land Incision* (1969) Oppenheim sought 'to correlate an incision in my wrist and the slow healing process with a cut or large ditch in the terrain' (Sharp 1971: 187–88). In *Arm and Wire* (1969), he went further, constructing the body as means, material and place of the work. This film, made with Bob Fiore, he recounts,

> incorporates a very close shot of my arm rolling across electrical cording, receiving the impression on the skin. Basically I make

no distinction between the material and the tool. The
impressions produced by the expenditure of downward pressure
are returned to their source and registered on the material that
expends the energy [. . .] *Arm and Wire* was an attempt to make
what you are making and *how* you are making it one and the same
thing. It consolidated output and compressed it into a single act.

(Sharp 1971: 187)

In this context, in introducing body art in the first issue of the influential journal *Avalanche* in 1970, the critic Willoughby Sharp
emphasised precisely this exchange, noting that 'The Body as Place is
a common condition of body works' where 'the body as place acts as
a ground which is marked' (Sharp 1970: 2). In Oppenheim's work, these
tautologies not only *act out* the body as a sculptural material, but transpose into performance a tactic incorporated into *Weight Displacement*.
Here, as part of his series of sculptural 'decompositions', Oppenheim
presented conic piles of the principal materials forming the walls and
floor of the gallery, so constituting a sculptural work out of the materials on which it rests. Announcing *Gallery Decomposition* (1969),
Oppenheim outlined the nature and consequences of this physical
erosion of the gallery building:

the material matter of my conic pile would be composed of
material ingredients of the supports on which it rests. Example:
A pile, leaning into a vertical wall support, spreading to the
ground, would be made of the ingredients of the supports
(gypsum, sand, cement, etc.). This allows the non-form to
'become the place' on which it rests [. . .] Decomposed form is
not put in place; it is that place.

(Oppenheim 1969)

This *undoing* of form, which Thomas McEvilley reads 'as a physical
demolition of the gallery [. . .] dissolving its walls to let in the outside
world' (McEvilley 1992: 16), is taken up in Oppenheim's performance.

In acting out '[t]he idea of the artist literally being *in* the material' (Sharp 1971: 186), Oppenheim performs the body as the site of the work, as if the work has become the place, and so the body, on which it rests. Here, Oppenheim states, 'I am creating a system that allows the artist to become the material, to consider himself the sole vehicle of the art, the distributor, initiator and receiver simultaneously' (Sharp 1971: 188). In doing so, however, Oppenheim not only fulfils a formal, sculptural imperative, but brings into play a series of *excessive* contents. Indeed, in setting out the consequences of acting as instrument and material, Oppenheim implies that his actions enter a realm notions of 'anti-form' or 'non-form' cannot readily embrace. Oppenheim notes that:

> Understanding the body as both subject and object permits one
> to think in terms of an entirely different surface. It creates a shift
> in direction from the creation of solid matter to the pursuit of an
> internal or surface change. With this economy of output one can
> oscillate from the position of instigator to victim.
>
> (Sharp 1971: 188)

In this sense, these approaches to the body work, like the *Gallery Decomposition*, 'to let the outside world in' (McEvilley 1992: 161) as an explicitly formal, sculptural logic generates implications and reversals which exceed its terms. Here, again, 'what bothers the order of things is that [. . .] there is not just a single order' (Zacharopolous 1996: 190), as Oppenheim acts out an explicitly sculptural process which realises implications and terms that cannot be held within its logic. In this respect, Oppenheim's approach to the body fulfils the impulse behind his documentations of actions on land. Where, as Oppenheim argues, land is 'not passive' (Oppenheim 1971: 188), the body's quintessential condition is *to be active* and to be *in activity*. In this sense, *Arm and Wire's* correspondence to *One Hour Run* extends toward its breaching of the aesthetic contexts and so formal containment its underlying sculptural logic implies. In this sense, body art, like land art, is rendered, in Oppenheim's practice, as constantly *in excess*.

For Acconci, too, the body in performance is always in exchange with interpenetrating and multiple systems of meaning. Like Oppenheim, Acconci performs the body as the means, material and place of the work, calling on an overtly formal and sculptural logic in his approach to the relations in which the work is established. Taking the 'notion of body as starting point' (*sic*) (Acconci 1972: 2), Acconci argues that since the body 'is a place it doesn't need a place' (Acconci 1972: 2). As the place of his work, though, the body always works against the condition of the object. In this context, the implications of Acconci's activities tend to exceed or slip beyond the overtly formal logic in which Acconci frames them. Acconci argues that

> One thing I learned through working with the body is that you
> can't think of it in terms of an object. I'm not interested in body
> as a sculptural thing at all. The body is not just there in relation
> to other things and to other physical spaces. The body is there in
> relation to memory, to all kinds of learning processes. There are
> all sorts of interconnections and connotations.
>
> (Nesmer 1971: 21)

For *Rubbing Piece*, an event at Max's Kansas City Restaurant in New York in May 1970, Acconci describes his 'project' as 'Sitting alone at a booth, during the ordinary activity at the restaurant. Rubbing my left forearm for one hour, gradually producing a sore' (Acconci 1996: 65). Here, Acconci acts out essentially the same circle of attention as Oppenheim in *Arm and Wire*. Thus, in his notes to the performance, he recounts a logic in which, as artist, he becomes 'Performer as producer (I give myself the sore); performer as consumer (I receive the sore)' and in which 'rather than do an act that takes place elsewhere, my body can be a place on which an event is enacted' (Acconci 1996: 65). Here, Acconci acts out his body as the material and place of the artwork, proposing that his performance 'consists in marking myself as performer: marking time' (Acconci 1996: 65). In this process, Acconci again works toward imbrications of public and private activities and spaces. In this private action in a public place, Acconci suggests, he creates a 'piece of biography that ordinarily would not have become part of one's active biography at all', where the exposure of the sore amounts to the 'exposure of a secret' (Acconci 1996: 65). Indeed, this exposure of a private act in a public work, Acconci supposes, produces 'performance as overlapping situations: one place in two different social occasions at one time' (Acconci 1996: 65).

This bringing of the private into the public, of the inside outside, is extended as Acconci focuses upon his own physical and psychological exposure as the material and place of a performed work. In *Trademarks* (1970), Acconci turns in on himself, biting different parts of his body in an effort to '[s]take a claim on what I have: the bite should be hard, should break down resistance: go through what I have' (Acconci 1972: 12). Here Acconci transposes a transition typical of site-specific installations and events on to his body as the place of the work, as he works to '[m]ake my own outside' and even to 'send my inside outside' (Acconci 1972: 9). In this way, and as if testing the proposition that there is a 'logic of materials', Acconci works to *reveal himself* in the material and place of the work. In performing, Acconci proposed in an interview of 1971,

> In order to make myself vulnerable I need strong attacks at the barriers [. . .] the shock aspect of my work is the result of an alarm reaction on my part to some external stimulus. I try to adapt to this external stimulus until I reach this exhaustion stage, where I can't resist anymore. The ultimate would be a complete death. [. . .] When you're in that exhausted stage you are out of control. You can't keep ordinary social forms. You are forced to break them because there's no way to handle them. If you use a strong stimulus, you can come closer to being exhausted. A lot of my work is concerned with exhaustion leading to an opening.
>
> (Nesmer 1971: 21)

In 'Adaptation Studies' (Acconci 1975), an essay and documentation concerning a cluster of filmed performances including *Blindfold Catching* (1970), *Soap and Eyes* (1970), and *Hand and Mouth* (1970), Acconci addresses the structure and effect of this process. In *Hand and Mouth* Acconci sets himself the task of attempting to force his whole hand into his mouth and so a task which will inevitably break down. Here, Acconci proposes, the action that takes him toward the goal, the forcing of his hand into his mouth, acts as a stress agent. As a response to the stress agent, the performance emerges and is carried forward, as his initial 'alarm reaction' and 'groping for direction' is overcome by his conscious adaptation. In this process, he states, 'when I choke and cough, I break my closed circle, slip into the viewer's region, lose my stance' (Acconci 1975: 195). Indeed, this process inevitably leads to the breakdown of the performance in the face of the stress and the impossible goal that will relieve it. Yet this is a breakdown which comes with Acconci's 'exhaustion', his arrival at a state where he has 'fallen to bits' under the exertion, under the pressure of attempting to adapt (Acconci 1975: 191). As *Hand and Mouth* continues so exhaustion sets in as, Acconci recalls, 'the more I do it, the worse I get – adaptation here can only mean that I'd have to be able to swallow my hand – pushing into myself results in pulling myself apart' (Acconci 1975: 194). Here, Acconci exposes himself as *agent*, and ground, of a performed work. In doing so, he *acts out* the body's resistances in an attempt to reveal *himself*, as social and psychological actor, as the site and material of the work. Here, performing the body as site implies, in much the same way as other approaches to site-specificity, a breaking down or dissolution of boundaries and limits, and *a forcing of the inside out*. 'Performing the body,' Acconci proposes, means 'making the body available – completing the body – bringing the body about' (Acconci 1972: 2).

It is finally this realisation of the body as a disordered, undisciplined site, a site of multiple, complex meanings, always in excess of the body-as-object, which both Acconci and Oppenheim attempt to act out through their entries into performance. Thus, in recounting the

development of his work from earth art to body art, Oppenheim recalls
that where:

> Earth Art was radical in the fact that in one gesture it countered
> major canons of traditional art, such as sellability, accessibility,
> mobility [. . .] Body Art had a far more substantial vein in which
> one could slowly build a case for art, for sculpture being able to
> survive and live within the dematerialised zone of psychological
> topology. And the kinds of persuasions and currents that an artist
> would succumb to and would be affected by within that
> dematerialised, sensory core, were really unknown. One was
> really throwing oneself to the wind.
>
> (Kaye 1996: 66)

In this work, the body is approached as an unstable site. Where,
Oppenheim proposes, '[o]ur bodies are constantly generating material,
building surfaces, changing physiognomy' (Sharp 1971: 188), body art
sets a sculptural work in a place in which it cannot rest. Indeed, in
these performances, the body reveals a place always *in process* and always
in excess of the work through which it might be seen.

Theatrical Materials: Station House Opera

Emerging, Julian Maynard Smith has suggested, 'out of minimal work
of the sixties and seventies' (Rogers 1988: 11–12), the British company
Station House Opera have developed performances which engage
with narrative, persona and dramatic continuity, and yet which play
out processes with explicitly sculptural or architectural imperatives. In
their breeze block performances beginning with *Jumpin' Jericho* of 1984,
the company have presented a series of works for theatres and other
sites articulated through relationships between found and constructed

architectures, objects, narratives and performance systems and processes. Indeed, Station House Opera frequently define their work in
the constraints ruling the performer's manipulation of the elements of
a structure to which he or she is subject, whether this be, as in *Drunken
Madness* of 1981, objects and other performers flighted in an unstable
system of interdependent platforms and pulleys (Maynard Smith 1996)
or the manipulation of a limited set of materials. For *The Bastille Dances*
of 1989, in which a breeze block edifice incorporating 8,000 blocks was
built and dismantled by a company of forty over a period of nine days,
performers' activities were caught between the demands of manipulating materials in a 'sculptural choreography' and the production of
complex dramatic images inviting, and displacing, readings of character,
narrative and incident.

In this context, the company engage with a performance style which
reflects their 'post-minimalist' (Rogers 1988: 11) origins, drawing on
the task-like or task-defined activity characterising aspects of post-
modern dance and early performance art. Maynard Smith recounts that
among the company's influences 'there were connections with Yvonne
Rainer and Trisha Brown, with the Judson Church Theatre' (Kaye 1996:
194). Of particular importance is Rainer's influential equation between
minimalist art and dance (Rainer 1974: 63) and Brown's exploration of
systemic processes, evident in her series of 'accumulation dances' of
the early 1970s in which the repetition and accumulation of a sequence
of actions reveals its ruling system or structure, as well as her task-
based 'equipment dances' of the late 1960s and early 1970s. For *Walking
Down the Side of a Building* (1969), Brown's performer walked down the
exterior façade of a skyscraper toward an audience at the foot of the
building, creating a powerful tension between the illusion of the walk
and the demands of the system of supports, lines and pulleys which
enabled the performance. For Anthony Howell, co-founder of The
Theatre of Mistakes in 1974, with whom Julian Maynard Smith and
Alison Urquhart performed before leaving to found Station House
Opera in 1980, an aesthetic closely linked to these post-minimal

practices defined the prevailing aesthetic of 'performance art'. In The Theatre of Mistakes, he recalls,

> Functionality was very important. Again and again during the evolution of the company the difference between dance and performance was stressed as essentially relating to the function of an action. A ballet dancer might jump in the air with his hands lifted, but a performance artist would jump up in the air to pull down a coat that was hung up on a branch – there was a function to the jump.
>
> (Kaye 1996: 133)

Station House Opera's work brings this tension between illusion and the 'physical givens' of performance, as well as concerns with 'functionality', to bear on explicitly theatrical spaces, structures and processes. In their early work, and under this aesthetic, the company sought to expose the physical limits of the theatre-site itself. In *Natural Disasters* (1980), *Drunken Madness* (1981), and *Cuckoo* (1984), all of which incorporated flying, Maynard Smith recalls:

> We wanted to occupy every part of the theatre – if it was proscenium, every part of the rectangle, every part of the whole space, equally [. . .] theatre has always been very conservative. It never takes into account its own physical limitations, which is one of the things we've always tried to do – to make theatre out of the physical limitations of the form. So we don't walk off in the wings. We're always physically stuck in that space.
>
> (Kaye 1996: 202)

Yet the company also extend this notion of the 'physical limitations' in which the performance is defined toward the various objects, relationships and systems they appropriate, and which create other kinds of physical contexts for the performer. Thus Maynard Smith argues that

with Station House, you could expand the notion of site to
include other things which are given. A site is just a physical
given – and it's not necessarily the building in which you're
doing it. We tend to work with lots of givens, because we take
things from the world and work with them. The breeze blocks
are a similar sort of given – it's 'site' in a sense. It's where you
locate your body in relation to how you manipulate it. And how
it manipulates you, as a physical thing.

(Kaye 1996: 201)

Just as these performances expose their 'physical' sites, so they also
explicitly engage with the viewer's reading of their significance. Here,
while focusing on the limitations and demands of the materials and
conditions confining and shaping their performance, the company *play
toward* the conventional theatrical sign. Thus, '[i]n the breeze block
pieces', Maynard Smith stresses, 'you would accept the breeze blocks –
accept their physical nature, not pretending they're something else –
but translate them into something more gestural, by wearing them, by
being expressive with them' (Kaye 1996: 195).

It is a logic which, for Maynard Smith, suggests that the objects and
systems the company appropriate retain some aspect of their 'identity',
appearing as 'found' even as they are displaced toward an articulation
of metaphor. In creating a context for performance explicitly defined
by these 'physical givens', Maynard Smith notes,

you must pay attention to its identity in your use of it [. . .]
That's the crucial thing all the way through. The table remains a
table even when it's 100 foot off the ground. It's still a table.
They're not 'made up' worlds, they are an assemblage of system
bits, but translated, somehow [. . .] when you use them in a
different way, when you put them in a different place – that's
what I mean by translating them.

(Kaye 1996: 201)

In this way, these performances not only work over their architectural spaces and appropriated objects and 'system bits' but, in this explicit translation, address the theatrical event as a site of metaphor. Noting that '[a]n audience always reads something fictional into the performance however un-dramatic you are trying to be' (Rogers 1988: 9–10), Maynard Smith remarks that Station House Opera have

> found it productive [. . .] to inhabit a kind of theatrical milieu while putting in this other stuff [. . .] to play with representation, with narrative – in a kind of fractured sense – to deliberately court that, to use those sorts of ambiguities. That's going to give you the duality of the performer as ordinary bloke and the performer as someone who is going to be read as being somebody.
>
> (Kaye 1996: 203)

It is a tension exemplified in the company's use of flying in performance, which, while permitting the performers to occupy every part of the space equally and so 'liberating the whole area of vision' (Rogers 1988: 12), explicitly invites metaphorical readings. Thus, in *Natural Disasters*, *Drunken Madness*, and *Cuckoo*, Maynard Smith remarks,

> All this escaping by flying – all the hanging tables – is precisely using the dual nature of what one might imagine is the ambition to fly. It's like the mental world of fantasy or ambition, and what happens when it comes up against the physical reality. Once you get someone off the ground they're incredibly heavy, which means you have to use all this technology. You find yourself with all these lumbering bits of cables and pulleys. And it's precisely that each of those informs the other. And gravity, obviously, becomes a central part of everything. That's why if you change the site the performance changes.
>
> (Kaye 1996: 202)

This tension is exacerbated in the relationship between these 'physical givens' and the narratives against which they are juxtaposed. Here, while these various 'appropriated' systems invite metaphorical readings, so narrative is treated as another object to be manipulated, allowing it to pass 'from person to person – and to thing, person to thing, thing to person' (Kaye 1996: 195). Indeed, it is in such exchanges that this work's site-specificity may be characterised. In relation to its sites, and whether or not it is staged in a theatre building, this performance operates in an exposure of the various 'physical limitations' defining performance and in the *effect* of the theatrical event itself, as these 'givens' are, by turn, *played toward* and *displaced from* symbolic significance. Here, where various 'fictions' alight on explicitly formal processes, only to be rendered as excessive, the company play out the proposition that '[a] word is not a concrete block' (Tschumi 1994d: 252). Under a logic of theatrical materials, however, Station House Opera locate their work in these very processes of translation, and so in the event in which these 'physical' sites are seen, through performance, to become the site of metaphor.

STATION HOUSE OPERA: THE BREEZE BLOCK PERFORMANCES

Jumpin' Jericho (1984) May '85 (1985) **A Split Second of Paradise** (1985) **Piranesi in New York** (1988) **The Bastille Dances** (1989) **Piranesi in Tokyo** (1990) **Piranesi in Melbourne** (1990) Dedesnn nn rrrrrr (1996) **The Salisbury Proverbs** (1997)

> **I:**   30 rehearsal photographs, from several hundred taken during rehearsals for **The Bastille Dances**.
>
> They portray a range of moments which became the recipe book of ideas for the sculptural choreography of the performance. The content of the photographs is simple and undramatic; it is the raw material from which the sequences and threads of the piece were made.

Breeze blocks were first used by SHO in **Jumpin' Jericho** as clothing for performers rooted to the ground, contrasting with others floating at tables and chairs in the air. Having to shift the blocks one by one limited movement and kept horizons earth-bound. They were strong and large enough to make architectonic, load-bearing structures, yet light enough to hold in one hand. They proposed a sculpturally defined world, and in the interplay between performers, a substitute for speech.

Everything follows from the simplicity and mobility of the blocks. Gesture, imprisonment, release, support, removal of support, enclosure, shelter, concealment, exposure, entombment, resurrection, bringing together, splitting apart, are simple functions of performers moving blocks in relation to each other.

The elements are combined in time and space: individuality and sociability, independence and interdependence, conflict and agreement, cruelty and compassion, are conjured up through manipulations of the same material. Dynamics, stillness, monumentality, instability, reversal and inversion, persistence and mutation, transformation and juxtaposition, coherence, chaos, collage, frequency, fluency, scale, geometry, blueprinted structures and structures as the undesigned result of performance rules, are combined in a spectacle which is completely open; the magic is that such dramatic changes can occur through a process taking place in front of the eyes.

II: The Salisbury Proverbs
A performance in 3 acts for 16 performers/singers, the Salisbury Festival
Chorus, live band and 8000 blocks.

The imprenetrable facade of a rocky domain inhabited by hermits and saints.

Down below, humans make a small impression on the landscape: statues, walls, furniture, a hut built on rubble. A poor material to work with, heavy and brittle; the imagination could have come up with something better.

The grass is cut and used to corral a pig. Above, she glides along on a pangolin. The pig becomes a statue.

Hearing her singing, he crashes through a wall. Another man falls through a wall behind him, gently this time, falling onto the bed the wall's made. The woman who had been peering around the corner finds herself in bed with him.

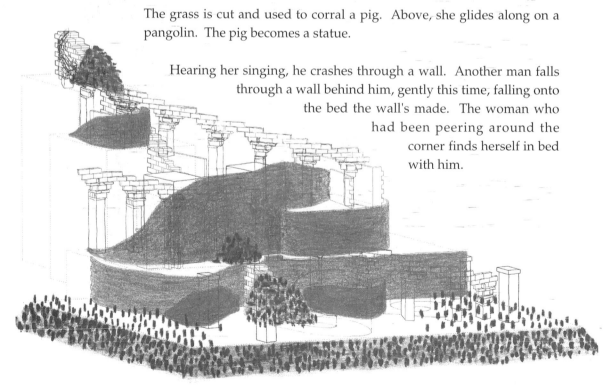

Behind them against a third wall is a falling man, upside down. In front, the first man is rescued only to be undermined. They're both wailing. He's saved from above by the object of his first interest.

She sits in a chair, reading. The bed moves; she will be caught yet.

The pangolin scrapes its rider off onto the wall.

Stuck in a wall for ages, she grinds a piece of broken block into a ball. It is thrown away. Below her a man is revealed also in a wall.

In front of him, a singing woman is put into a tower. From under the pile of rubble used for building it emerges a singing man.

The cliff face is breached and squared into a grand arch. A cathedral is formed, a rising central nave with multiple transepts.

Into this symmetrical and hierarchical space with its staircase leading up to the cathedral spire, come disturbances...

The man in the wall is unbuilt by the Virgin Mary who clasps his limp body to her chest. On the other side, another deposition, derived from a brawl. Two piétas, one born from order and the other from chaos, one ending in resurrection and the other in a coffin: a success rate of 50%.

He walks off the edge. Climbing back up the stairs, he is half-swallowed by them. Pulled out, he is thrown further down. Above him, she dives from the wall and a bath appears. Her cat becomes a book and is read from. As she relaxes, a hand comes through the wall to caress her face. She is overcome and the wall becomes her tomb.

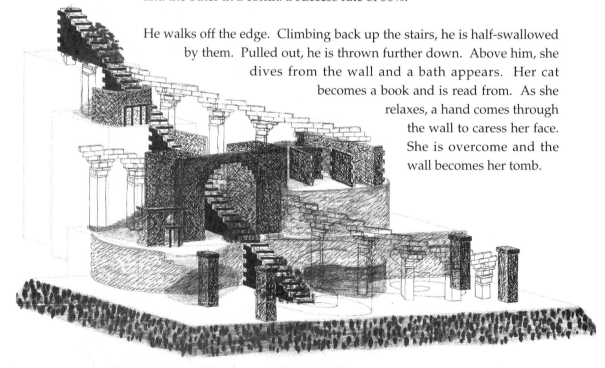

She skateboards down the
staircase. At the bottom she
catapults into the long table,
turning it into a giant splash.
She is frozen for a long time.

Like all spectacles, the distant
view has more impression
than substance. Only when a
block is dropped is the weight
understood. Only when a wall
collapses is danger apparent.

Everything strives for a single image of harmony, yet this focus is split; aside from the local irregularities – victims in towers, colliding walls, corridors and furniture, a prison where the pulpit should be – there is a more basic instability, a discordance in the geometry, two close but clashing axes, with an insidious, whispering interchange of forms.

The cathedral is transformed; a baroque disease spreads spiralling systems of arches throughout the space. The focus disappears. The great arch is reduced to two broken stumps.

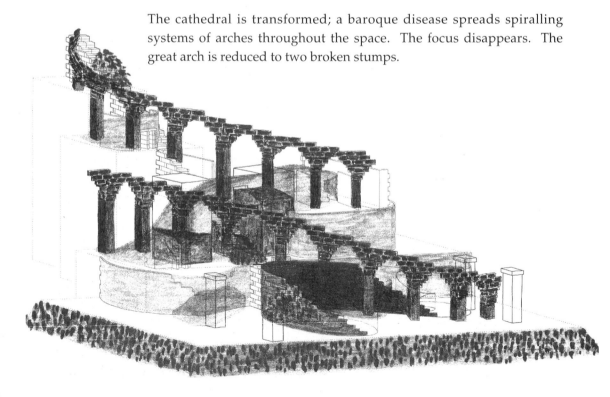

A tower is dismantled, the blocks being thrown onto a writhing man to bury him. A singing man is revealed.

An ark appears on top of the mountain. Meanwhile, the erstwhile bathroom has become the Pope's room. The furniture eats itself, chasing itself around the floor. A corner nudges a drum and leaves its imprint.

A wall uncoils and traverses the floor, interleaving with the spiral arches. It coils back again, turning the inside outside, inverting the space. A human vortex appears at its centre. The Pope moons from his window (echoes of the pig).

On the mountain a burning bush is rearranged as a fiery table and chair. Flaming blocks are recycled into a row of dominoes which are kicked over, setting the scene on fire.

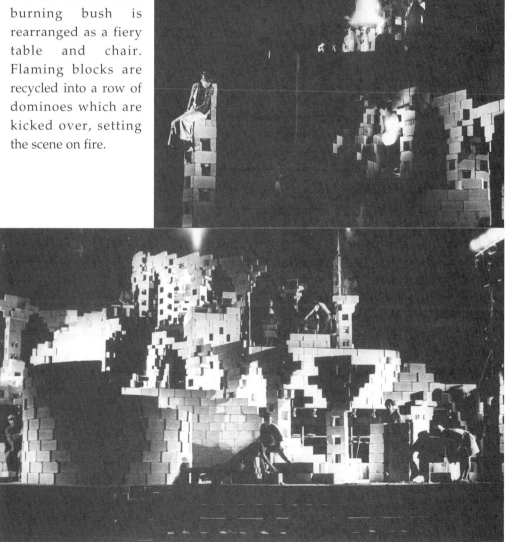

Frames

The Outside ✗ the Inside.

(Derrida 1974: 44)

Where site-specificity arises in a disturbance of the opposition between 'virtual' and 'real' spaces, in dialectical relationships between the work and its site, or in a questioning of the art object's material integrity, so the very possibility of establishing a work's proper location is called into question. Indeed, here, site-specificity is linked not only to a transitive definition of site but, more broadly, to shifts in visual art toward the conceptual and performative contexts in which the *idea* of the work is defined. For Miwon Kwon, writing of 'One Place After Another: Notes on Site Specificity' (Kwon 1997), this development is reflected in certain paradigmatic concepts of site where, Kwon proposes, 'in advanced art practices of the past thirty years the operative definition of the site has been transformed from a physical location – grounded, fixed, actual – to a discursive vector – ungrounded, fluid, virtual' (Kwon 1997: 95). Here, where the site functions as a text perpetually in the process of being written and being read, then the site-specific work's very attempt to establish its place will be subject to the process of slippage, deferral and indeterminacy in which its signs are constituted. Yet although Kwon identifies this discursive paradigm (Kwon 1997: 95) with more recent art practice, its basis lies in approaches to site which are contemporaneous with minimalism, and which further elaborate the link between site-specificity and performance.

Repetition and Location: Daniel Buren

Since 1965, the French artist Daniel Buren has worked systematically to define his practice in terms of a single, ostensibly simple form, in whose repetition he might address the artwork's construction in relation to multiple discourses. Buren's practice is indebted to the work of the French Dadaist Marcel Duchamp, whose series of 'Ready-mades', produced between 1914 and 1917, address the reading of the object through the conceptual frames implied by the gallery. In presenting such objects as *Bottle Dryer* (1914), a snow shovel under the title *The Advance of the Broken Arm* (1914) and an upturned urinal as *Fountain* (1917), Duchamp used paradox to expose the role of the specific site in the viewer's negotiation over identity and meaning. For Duchamp, it seems, the very banality of the largely unaltered, functional objects he chose to sign, date and present in the gallery as Ready-mades, served, first of all, to challenge the viewer's reading of his gesture. Speaking 'Apropos of Ready-mades' in New York in 1961, at the time of his resurgent influence on new art and performance, Duchamp argued that he had deliberately placed objects of little or no 'aesthetic' value before the viewer, emphasising that 'the choice of these "Ready-Mades" was never dictated by aesthetic delectation. This choice was based on a reaction of visual indifference with at the same time a total absence of good or bad taste [. . .] in fact a complete anaesthesia' (Sanouillet and Peterson 1975: 141).

While Duchamp's placement of the object in the gallery invokes the terms of sculpture, the efficacy of his gesture lies in the object's resistance, in the eyes of the viewer, to the terms through which it is presented. Here, where these everyday, banal objects are denaturalised by being placed in the gallery, yet remain, in some aspect, outside of the conventional terms of sculpture, they might provoke the viewer's awareness of her own reading towards a work. In this event, the Ready-made occurs in an unsteady blocking together of conflicting identities, in a tension, a vacillation, in looking, where it becomes apparent that the identity of the object can be resolved only in the viewer's performance of its terms. In this sense, the Ready-made arises in the viewer's own sense of indeterminacy, of doubt, with regard to the terms and limits of that which is seen.

Like Duchamp's Ready-mades, Buren's practice is explicitly designed to exceed and subvert the conventional terms in which it may be read, conceding the ephemerality of the work and implicating the viewer in its completion. Yet Buren's practice is implicitly critical of Duchamp's placement of found material, and defines a more sustained, critical address to the ideological sites in which the work is produced.

Since 1965, Buren has developed his presentations through the elaboration of an apparently simple visual scheme in a wide variety of differing circumstances and locations. Subject in its development, he suggests, to 'no research' (Buren 1973: 12) and betraying '**no formal evolution** – even though there is change' (Buren 1973: 16), Buren has offered the systematic playing out of his scheme on gallery walls, architectural façades, private buildings, transportation spaces, within public squares, on advertising hoardings, as well as in book-works, and through peripatetic street demonstrations or 'ballets'. All these presentations, he reports, are manifestations of a strategy whereby

> Vertically striped sheets of paper, the bands of which are 8.7 cms. wide, alternate white and coloured, are stuck over internal and external surfaces: walls, fences, display windows, etc.; and/or cloth/canvas support, vertical stripes, white and coloured bands each 8.7 cms., the two ends covered with dull white paint.
>
> (Buren 1973: 12)

Buren's installation of these vertical bands which are 'always the same $[x,y,x,y,x,y,x,y,x,y,x \ldots]$' (Buren 1973: 13) is defined in a rejection of the development, or even variation, of terms through which the formal or stylistic development of his work might conventionally be read. Where, as Buren suggests, contradictions are removed from 'the internal structure of the proposition' such that 'no "tragedy" occurs on the reading surface, no horizontal line, for example, chances to cut through a vertical line' (Buren 1973: 14) then it might become apparent that for Buren '**formal problems have ceased to interest us**' (original emphasis) (Buren 1973: 14). Indeed, these installations not only work against readings of a formal progression from one work to another, but also a resolution of Buren's activity into readings of a single, formally autonomous work reproduced in differing locations. To this end, Buren's 'method of work' (Buren 1973: 12) is not only to repeat the installation of the vertical bands but to arbitrarily vary and expose the distinctions and limits defining each display. Here, in '**a repetition of differences with a view to the same (thing)**' (*sic*) (Buren 1973: 17), Buren continually resets arbitrary limits around these vertical bands in an attempt to produce 'a minimum or zero or neutral composition' (Buren 1973: 13). It is a set of strategies, Buren argues, which results in a 'formal neutrality', a neutrality which 'would not be formal at all if the internal structure [. . .] (vertical white and colored bands) was linked to the external form (size of the surface presented to view)' (Buren 1973: 14). He concludes:

> The internal structure being immutable, if the exterior form were equally so, one would soon arrive at the creation of a quasi-religious archetype which, instead of being neutral, would become burdened with a whole weight of meanings, one of which – and not the least – would be the idealized image of neutrality.
>
> (Buren 1973: 14)

As this suggests, Buren conceives of his method of work as posing, first of all, *the question* of how these vertical bands might be read. Where the realisation of an idealised image of neutrality would assume a stable formal identity, this *formal neutrality* suggests an evasion of familiar or available readings in a displacement of conventional forms. Thus, while Buren explicitly presents his activity in relation to familiar practices, his method systematically counters the formal readings these relationships invite. In defining a flat, painted surface which eschews illusion and representation, then, Buren's displays invite comparison to abstract painting, even to the work of those Modernist painters who, at the time of his first activities, had been read as excising that which is 'unessential' to the medium in a programmatic reduction of painting to its 'formal essence' (Fried 1968, Greenberg 1962). Evidently for Buren, though, far from entrenching his activity within painting, his method poses the question of these bands' relation to painting, so engaging critically with such essentialist notions. To determine his work 'as painting', Buren argues, is 'like finding a solution without answering the question. Not to say that my work is not possible to classify, but you cannot, certainly, say it's painting. What painter will accept that, anyhow? [. . .] then you have to say it's sculpture also' (White 1979: 9).

Indeed, Buren's presentations might more appropriately be read as analogous to minimalism's extreme formal simplicity, with its consequent deferral of attention toward the literal circumstances in which the object is encountered. Faced with the repetition of Buren's 'immutable' internal structure, it follows, the viewer's attention might be deflected toward the 'objecthood' (Fried 1968) of the two-dimensional picture-plane, an objecthood Buren articulates through his arbitrary variation of the external form of each presentation. Yet, for Buren, it seems that this relationship is equally equivocal. Reading minimalist sculpture as 'idealist' and 'uncritical' (Buren 1973: 43), he argues that such objects exemplify a contradiction between the impulse 'to use raw material which *a priori* has no front or back (a steel plate, a wooden plank . . .)' and its subsequent transformation

> into a box, cube or simple volume – thus immediately creating a
> recto and a verso, a visible side (the body) and a hidden one (the
> soul) [. . .] The resulting object can be defined as typically
> idealistic, since one pretends to ignore what is really at work.
>
> (Buren 1973: 44)

While the unitary forms' address to space and the experience of the viewer can be seen as precisely a function of this duality, of a tension between that which can be seen and that which the object hides or obscures, Buren supposes that these vertical bands pose the question of what remains where 'the total absence of conflict eliminates all conceal-ment' (Buren 1973: 14). In this sense, Buren's 'work' might be identified with a series of propositions, each of which remains open to question. In proposing a relation to painting, Buren's elimination of visual inci-dent and programmatic variation of external form defers the viewer to its objecthood. Yet, in proposing an incursion into sculpture, the very two-dimensionality of the painted surface defers back to the condition of painting. Indeed, in this context, what remains, where this zero or neutral composition takes effect, are precisely *questions* of formal status and location.

Yet, in order to keep such questions open, Buren's method must also work against the possibility of its own synthesis or transcendence of the practices to which it refers. In this respect, Buren's method estab-lishes a characteristic tension, where the emphatic repetition of a particular form is articulated through procedures which *work against* the very values of originality, uniqueness and permanence by which an artwork is conventionally established and where, in subverting the claim, if only by default, to be offering its own unique and autonomous terms, '[t]he repetition of a neutral form [. . .] does not lay emphasis upon the work, but rather tends to efface it' (Buren 1973: 19).

In this context, where a variation of external form 'fragments the aforementioned work into as many occasions as there are places used' (Buren 1973: 6), giving rise to 'the appearance of [. . .] profuseness and ephemerality' (Buren 1973: 18), Buren's work is *dispersed* across a series of displays, each of which 'cannot be moved elsewhere and will have to disappear at the end of its exhibition' (Buren 1973: 5). Such 'disap-pearance through destruction', Buren argues, 'opens a breach in the dominant artistic ideology which wants a work to be immortal and therefore indestructible' (Buren 1973: 5). Furthermore, where these arbitrary permutations demonstrate that 'the external form (shifting) has no effect on the internal structure' (Buren 1973: 16), this method works against the very *singularity* of the variations it produces. Where it becomes evident to the viewer that 'the external size is arbitrary',

Buren supposes, it might also be clear that 'delimitation of the work at the top and at the bottom [. . .] "exists" only by mental reconstruction', with the result that it 'is mentally demolished simultaneously' (Buren 1973: 14). Here, where the very *differences* through which the viewer might ascribe significance to these 'individual' works are put under erasure, Buren effects 'the endless canceling-out or the disappearance of form itself, the ceaseless posing of the question of its presence; and thence of its disappearance' (Buren 1973: 18).

Here it becomes clear that Buren's method is dedicated to a systematic undermining of the very status, identity and significance of that which it produces. Indeed, even in its address to the 'problem' of 'how to dispose of the object' (Buren 1973: 11), this method works against the simple dissolution of conventional form, where the object might be substituted by an idea. Buren observes that

> To exhibit a 'concept' or to use the word concept to signify
> art, comes to the same thing as putting the concept itself on a
> level with the object. This would be to suggest that we must
> think in terms of a 'concept-object' – which would be an
> aberration.
>
> (Buren 1973: 11)

Thus Buren's emphatic repetition of these vertical bands asserts the *materiality* of the picture-plane, just as it threatens to *cancel out* its significance, effecting not so much the 'de-materialization' of the object, as **'the object questioning its own disappearance as object'** (Buren 1976). Indeed, in this context, Buren's method reproduces much the same critical relationship to the dematerialised realm of conceptual art as to painting and sculpture, as it entertains 'two apparently contradictory considerations: on the one hand, the reality of a certain form [. . .] and on the other hand, its **canceling out** by successive and identical confrontations' (Buren 1973: 25).

Yet, caught in this process of erasure, where the work cannot readily be located in terms of any one of the forms or practices to which it refers, or even as an autonomous work which transcends these references, what remains is precisely *the problem of locating* that which Buren produces. Paradoxically, though, it is here that Buren's method addresses the site of the work, for, Buren supposes, it is in this problem of location that the conceptual, discursive and ideological sites of the work's production might be seen. If the work could be located, *the question of its presence* would be resolved or answered. In this sense, and after Buren, it is possible to conclude that 'paradoxically: the proposition in question "has no real location"' (Buren 1973: 20), for this proposition arises *in* the very problem of locating, and so establishing, the terms of a work. What remains under these circumstances is *the question* of the work's production, *the question* of its location.

Like Duchamp, Buren's practice invokes a series of spaces and forms already coded, and which provide the site and context for his own activity. Also like Duchamp, his practice aims toward an equivocal and unstable critical engagement with these spaces, in which he pursues a systematic resistance to formal closure. Indeed, here, the space which practice enters, as the architectural critic Anthony Vidler suggests in relation to Vito Acconci's work, 'is considered to be an already occupied terrain' (Acconci 1993: 37). It is in this context that Duchamp attempts to interrupt or puncture the discourses in which the art object is constituted. Here, in bringing the conventions of one location to bear upon another, Douglas Crimp concludes:

> Duchamp's readymades [. . .] embodied the proposition that the artist invents nothing, that he or she only uses, manipulates, displaces, reformulates, repositions what history has provided. [. . .] The readymades propose that the artist cannot *make*, but can only *take* what is already there.
>
> (Crimp 1993: 71)

It is in this sense that Duchamp reveals the history and ideology of the art object, as it is constructed through the gallery, to be the *site* of his work.

Yet Duchamp's practice also suggests a specific limit to the Ready-made's interrogation of the gallery as a site. In functioning *inside* the museum, through the physical relocation of an everyday object, the Ready-made threatens to conflate the work of art's formal and physical location. Furthermore, in constructing an opposition between an everyday, utilitarian object and an aesthetic frame belonging to the gallery, the Ready-made risks capitulation. Indeed, this is another implication of the Ready-made's address to site: that the gallery is a place of transformation, where either the utilitarian object can acquire the aesthetic mantle of the art object, or where a conceptual turn in art may supersede and transcend the banality of the everyday. Here, the question posed by the Ready-made is resolved into sculpture.

It is in these contexts that Buren proposes that not only must the site be revealed as implying the identity of the art object, but the object must act as a critical mirror to the ground on which it stands. Acknowledging that '[e]very place radically imbues (formally, architecturally, sociologically, politically) with its meaning the object (work creation) shown there', Buren proposes that '[t]o reveal this limit (this role), the object presented and its place of display must dialectically imply one another' (Buren 1976). Here, Buren approaches the museum as a conceptual framework rather than a built form, in an attempt to reveal not only the site's definition of the work, but the work's definition of its site. Here, where 'the location (outside or inside) where a work is seen is its frame (its **boundary**)' (Buren 1973: 21), Buren's use of locations *outside* the museum reveals that his method of work, through its equivocal relationships with other art practices, implies the frame of the gallery or the museum. In contrast to Duchamp, Buren's 'object' reveals itself to be *produced* and so *penetrated* by the conceptual frameworks of the gallery, such that 'it is possible to go outside the cultural location in the primary sense (gallery, museum, catalogue...) without the proposition, considered as such, immediately giving way' (Buren 1973: 20–21). In this way, too, Buren proposes that the gallery functions, firstly, as a conceptual and discursive site. Indeed, Buren works to reduce or 'neutralise' the form of his work, and disperse his activity, to such a point that 'under the threat of permanently reducing the work to nothing' (Buren 1976), the conceptual frame which these vertical bands imply might come into restless play with Buren's practice.

Here, too, the relationship between Buren's method and the art practices to which it refers becomes clear. In so far as Buren's method presents itself in relation to painting, for example, it does not present the installation of these vertical bands 'as painting', but with regard to the *system of painting*, as a context, a support, in its organisation of meaning. Here, Buren's zero or neutral composition serves, through its repetition, to assert a troubled and critical relationship to painting as a system which *produces* 'art objects,' and which constitutes one of its sites. Thus, where 'painting' addresses 'the system of painting' as its *site*, Buren asserts, it should no longer be concerned with 'the vague vision/illusion' but with the '**VISUALITY of the painting itself.** [. . .] painting itself should create a mode, a specific system, which would no longer direct attention, but which is "produced to be looked at"' (Buren 1973: 13). Painting as a practice, in other words, should present itself as a naming, and a questioning, of the 'specific system' in which it is constituted, and so in a revelation of the ground on which it stands.

'Framing and Being Framed'*: Hans Haacke

Buren's address to the discourses in which the work is constituted reveals the limits and boundaries of the artwork to be inescapably *restless*. Here, where the artwork is defined in a set of framing conditions it dialectically implies, then the 'inside' of the work is always already penetrated by the outside. It follows that a reading of the artwork implies a continual deferral between 'inside' and 'outside', and

---

* This subtitle is taken from the title of Hans Haacke's book, *Framing and Being Framed: 7 Works*, published in Halifax, Nova Scotia in 1975 by the Nova Scotia College of Art and Design.

so movement between a given practice and its discursive sites. Indeed, while Buren stresses that, '[a]rchitecture of any sort is in fact the inevitable background, support and frame of any work' (White 1979: 19), the architecture toward which Buren directs attention is one defined conceptually and textually, even as it is *built*. Arguing against 'the pseudo-freedom' of the pretext that a work 'can be transported from here to there, anywhere, from one exhibition to another, regardless of the architecture of the place in which it is displayed' (Buren 1976), Buren goes on to conclude that:

> The architecture of a gallery, in which the work must take shape,
> is perhaps not only the actual exhibition room (where the goods
> are shown), but also the director's office (where the goods are
> sold), the store-room (where the goods are kept), the reception
> room (where the goods are discussed). It is perhaps also the
> external architecture of the gallery, the staircase up to it, or
> the lift, the street leading to it, the area where it is situated, the
> town.
>
> (Buren 1976)

In Hans Haacke's later work, in which he extends his concept of 'real-time systems' from inorganic and biological processes toward the social and political relationships underpinning the authority of the museum, the site-specific work exposes the very institutional conditions under which it operates. Working on the premise, the critic Jack Burnham reports, that 'all galleries and museums function under specific ideological constraints' (Burnham 1975: 136), Haacke proceeds to document 'real-time' social systems, relations and processes which are *in operation* through the gallery. Presented without commentary, and reproducing publicly available records, Burnham observes that Haacke's interventions do not simply *represent* a set of relationships, but expose their own implication in the 'real' systems they describe. In this way, Burnham concludes, Haacke is one of a number of artists who attempt to integrate their works into the actual events of the 'real world,' that is the world of politics, money-making, ecology, industry, and other pursuits. In effect the work becomes not only the original concept or piece, but any significant public or official response to it, or any further variations which the work may take as a result of its engagement with the world-at-large.

(Burnham 1975: 133)

The uneasy nature of this exchange is characterised in the title under which Haacke documents these works: *Framing and Being Framed* (Haacke 1975). In exposing the institutional relationships in which it functions, these works frame the very terms in which they are them-selves *being framed*, threatening to implicate themselves in the very moment they incriminate the gallery or museum. In this paradoxical intervention into its own ideological and political sites, Rosalyn Deutsche argues, work such as this

broadened the concept of site to embrace not only the aesthetic context of a work's exhibition but the site's symbolic, social, and political meanings as well as the historical circumstances within which artwork, spectator and place are situated.

(Deutsche 1996: 162)

Indeed, in its development, Haacke's project has unfolded in a systematic address to the constraints acting upon the gallery, the viewer, and the object, and in which it is constituted as a work. In *MOMA Poll*, for the Information show at the Museum of Modern Art, New York in June to September 1970, Haacke proposed that his work should consist of an ongoing exhibition of the results of a poll in which

visitors were requested to answer an either-or question referring to a current socio-political issue. They would cast a ballot onto one of two transparent ballot boxes marked respectively 'yes' or

'no' [. . .] I did not hand in the question until the evening before
the opening of the exhibition.

(Haacke 1975: 9)

For the John Weber Gallery in 1972 and 1973, Haacke produced a
series of detailed statistical profiles of the audience visiting the work,
implying an ongoing process in which the site-specific work consists of
a record of the conditions of its reception. For *John Weber Gallery
Visitors' Profile 2* of 1973

> the visitors of the show were requested to answer 21 multiple
> choice questions, printed on both sides of a key sort card, by
> punching out the answers of their choice. The questions inquired
> about the visitor's demographic background and opinions on
> socio-political and art issues. The questionnaires were provided
> in 2 file trays sitting on either end of a long table in the centre of
> the exhibition. Punchers were hanging from the ceiling above the
> table. The punched cards were to be dropped into a wooden box
> with a slit in the top. Throughout the exhibition intermediate
> results of the new survey were posted as part of the show.

(Haacke 1975: 41)

For *Seurat's 'Les Poseuses' (small version), 1888–1975* Haacke presented
fourteen panels shown at the John Weber Gallery in May 1975, setting
out a record of the increasing value of the Seurat painting against
the details of its ownership, including the personal, business and
known political affiliations of its owners. Most notoriously, in *Shapolsky
et al. Manhattan Real Estate Holdings, a Real-Time Social System, as
of May 1, 1971* and *Sol Goldman and Alex DiLorenzo Manhattan Real
Estate Holdings, a Real-Time Social System, as of May 1, 1971*, created for
his first one-person show at the Guggenheim Museum, New York
in 1971, Haacke proposed to reproduce public records in order to
document

the property holdings and investment activities of two separate real-estate groups. One piece provided information about various types of buildings owned by the association of Sol Goldman and Alex DiLorenzo. The other displayed the slum properties of the Shapolsky family organisation.

(Deutsche 1996: 168)

Here, Deutsche reports, Haacke presented 'individual photographs of 142 buildings and vacant lots located primarily in New York slum neighbourhoods as well as a number of typewritten sheets, charts, diagrams, and maps detailing real-estate transactions' (Deutsche 1996: 169). On the grounds of its very social and political specificity, however, these works prompted the Guggenheim Director's cancellation of Haacke's exhibition a matter of weeks before its planned opening in April 1971 (Deutsche 1996: 165). Commenting on Haacke's allegations of 'social malpractice', the Director objected specifically to Haacke's naming and so public exposure of 'individuals and companies whom you consider at fault' (Deutsche 1996: 168). As Deutsche observes, however, Haacke's real-time system reproduces information already in the public domain. The Guggenheim's concern, she concludes, was that in housing 'representations of buildings defined solely as economic entities [. . .] the museum might have emerged as a space occupying a position of material privilege in relation to other sites' (Deutsche 1996: 171).

For Frederic Jameson, Haacke's address to real-time social systems defining such institutions' authority and position represents a specific extension of the tactics of conceptual art toward a cognitive mapping of art's infrastructure. Here, he proposes, Haacke 'redirects the deconstruction of perceptual categories specifically onto the framing institution', deferring attention from the museum space and toward 'the museum itself' which

as an institution, opens up into its network of trustees, their affiliations with multinational corporations, and finally the global system of late capitalism proper, such that what used to be the limited and Kantian project of a restricted conceptual art expands into the very ambition of cognitive mapping itself (with all its specific representational contradictions).

(Jameson 1991: 158)

Indeed, while Haacke opens up the institutions of art in this mapping, so his work also foregrounds the contradictions of its own ambivalent position. Where, as Jameson points out, Haacke's 'situation-specific' work 'foregrounds the museum as such and its institutionality' (Jameson 1991: 162), so as Howard S. Becker and John Walton point out in considering 'Social Science and the Work of Hans Haacke', 'Haacke works in the same social space as those his work describes' (Becker & Walton 1975: 151). Here, in mapping the 'specific ideological constraints' of the museum as a social institution, Haacke's work participates in, and is conditioned by, the paradox of approaching the site *of* the work *through* the work. Thus, in this exposure of the museum, Jameson proposes, Haacke attempts 'to transform the "extrinsic" determinants of art into the "intrinsic" content of a new artistic text' (Jameson 1986: 49). In doing so, he concludes, this work vacillates between possibilities. On the one hand, Haacke's documentation of the social and political conditions in which his work functions threatens to abolish the artwork in the attempt to reveal its site. Here, Jameson points out, and as distinct from other, more formal engagements with site-specificity, 'what survives the extinction of the "work" is not its materials or components, but rather something very different, its presuppositions, its conditions of possibility' (Jameson 1986: 43). On the other hand, Haacke's work implicates itself, as 'work of art', in the very relations and processes it critiques. Indeed, Burnham points toward an analogous 'oscillation' in Haacke's early work. Here, in presenting self-contained, self-explanatory inorganic, organic, or biological systems in the gallery, such as *Double-Decker Rain* (1963) and *Grass Grows* (1967), and despite his refusal through the system to make any overt or specific reference to 'art', Burnham argues 'their fine arts context allows them to share the cultural overtones of their environment. According to Haacke, this produces in the viewer's mind a condition of conceptual oscillation [. . .] For Haacke, this irresolution remains of prime importance' (Burnham 1975: 132).

For Jameson, this irresolution seems evident in Haacke's approach to the museum, even as he engages in a cognitive mapping of the museum as institution. Thus, Jameson argues, Haacke's 'situation-specific' practice is caught in

> the uneasy gestalt alternation between a 'work of art' that
> abolishes itself to disclose the museum structure which contains it
> and one that expands its authority to include not merely that
> institutional structure but the institutional totality in which it is
> itself subsumed.
>
> (Jameson 1991: 158)

Here, as elsewhere, the relationship of the map to its site is paradoxical and restless. In Haacke's work, specifically in *framing and being framed*, the site-specific work threatens to transform the very sites it acts as an index to, even as it works to expose and foreground the social and political 'conditions of its possibility' (Jameson 1991: 43).

Yet, in this respect, the irresolution in Haacke's work echoes a restlessness which is fundamental to site-specificity itself. Indeed, it is in response to the capacity of a 'site-specific work' to transform the very sites it seeks to expose that the practices considered in this volume so frequently define explicitly *restless* and *unresolved* exchanges and processes. It is in this restlessness, too, that site-specificity defers to the terms and practices of *performance*, even as it presents itself in relation to explicitly architectural, sculptural, or object-based modes of work. Thus, for Buren and Haacke, this formal 'irresolution' or 'uneasy gestalt' implicates the viewer in a process of *locating* the limits of their practice, and so in mapping and producing its sites, precisely in order to expose a place always already being *acted out*.

Performing Inside and Outside: Fiona Templeton

This 'irresolution' finds its counterpart in site-specific theatre, where the limits and inter-dependence of work and site frequently come under question. Such an 'irresolution', and an exposure of performance as 'framing and being framed', is clearly at play in work by Oldenburg, Kaprow and Meredith Monk, even as this work departs radically from the concerns of Buren and Haacke. The British artist Fiona Templeton's site-specific work *YOU – The City* (1988) has similarly addressed the limits of work and site, and so a *performance* of site-specificity. Constructed as 'an intimate Manhattan-wide play for an audience of one' in the form of 'a journey through both known and obscure parts of the city' (Templeton 1990: ix), *YOU – The City* offers its 'clients' guided tours of Manhattan through twenty or more locations hosted by a series of performers. Addressed directly by each performer through a flow of text that turns on the word 'you', *YOU – The City* confronts each client with a 'radically interactive' 'play' (Templeton 1990: ix) where conventional oppositions between performance and environment, performer and spectator, are continually challenged. Recounting his response to its later realisation in London, Tim Etchells suggests that

> The old dialectical separations between inside and outside, fiction and reality, self and other, audience and performer, were here exploited and blurred, leaving the strange sense that the city and oneself were now almost the same thing, a shifting network of narratives, places, touches, voices, lost puns, myths and intimacies.
>
> (Etchells 1994: 119)

In her 'Afterword' to the performance, Templeton recalls the articulation of relationships between performer and client not only through this text, but in the playing of cinematic conceits through live performance, where a non-theatrical location provides the possibilities of long-shot, including the performer's choosing to frame him or herself against a close-up or distant background [. . .] close-up is reclaimed in YOU from the automatic seduction of spectacle and replaced into presence, live responsibility, theatre in your face.

(Templeton 1990: 141)

In *YOU – The City*, not only are the oppositions which Etchells identifies implicitly under question, but at its culmination the client's implication in the construction of the work is brought into sharp focus. In Act IV scene iii, the 'climax of the piece' (Templeton 1990: 143), the client finds herself back in the place of an earlier scene, a playground, where, as a 'less advanced client', she had walked towards and crossed the path of a 'performer'. Now, though, the client discovers herself *being seen* in the role of 'performer', as she faces an oncoming client moving through the earlier scene. Here, Templeton suggests

a revelation and a certain power are yours: it is on being made to wait for the client on the far side that you realise, if you had not already been warned by the fact that the pronoun 'you' [. . .] has suddenly disappeared from the text [. . .] that you can now be a performer in any way whatsoever to the approaching client, including choosing to admit to the identity of the client, which the less advanced one may or may not be willing now to believe.

(Templeton 1990: ix–x)

In this moment, the 'advanced client' is subject to a blocking together, around her own presence, of the roles of 'client' and 'performer'. Entrapped into seeing herself *act out* the work, the client discovers herself at once *inside* the piece, as performer, and *outside*, as a witness to its effect. Like Duchamp's Ready-made, this effect rests upon the viewer's awareness of an opposition, here 'performer' and 'viewer', at the very moment in which its construction is revealed to be contingent upon her looking. In this way, *YOU – The City* sets a conceptual trap, in which the client becomes witness, to herself, in the act of *performing* the oppositions in which the work is defined. Indeed, in this moment, Templeton's site-specific performance reveals its deferral from inside to outside, as, in its positioning of the viewer, it at once constructs, exposes, and upsets its own limits.

Meredith Monk

"I sometimes think that one of the beauties of live performance is that it ignites a space and time and then disappears." — Meredith Monk

Since the late 1960's Monk has been a pioneer in the making of site-specific work, often presenting her visionary music/movement/theater pieces in nontraditional locations. Free from the limitations of theater stages, lighting, and acoustics, she has explored a broad range of possibilities in these pieces, always combining disciplines and introducing elements unexpected in the performance arena such as boats, live animals, motorcycles, arc welders, armies and fire. Ideas central to much of her site-specific work have been the notions of scale, time, and their transformation. Monk chooses her sites carefully, often likening her role in the creation of her work to that of an archeologist in order, as she has said, "to excavate a space and let it speak."

— Siri Engberg

Informational Placards
from the exhibit,
Art Performs Life,
Walker Art Center, 1998

When I came to New York, I performed mostly in galleries and on proscenium stages. At the same time, I was very interested in space and new ways of dealing with the performer-audience relationship. In Break, the first piece that I presented in New York, I ran out into the audience at a certain point in the continuity, looking back with them at the empty space. I liked the idea of the absence of figure and the awareness of the space itself within a piece. By 1966, I was dissatisfied with frontal stage orientation and began working out some of my ideas by teaching workshops in various sites in New York City: Battery Park, the subway, abandoned factories and the Staten Island Ferry to name a few. Each class became an urban expedition.

— Meredith Monk

Alfred North
pouring 50 lbs of flour
from the roof of
the building.

Blueprint

1967, Site: A five story building,
Group 212, Woodstock, New York.
For 10 performers.

In 1967, I presented my first outdoor site-specific work, Blueprint. It took place in a five story building with the audience sitting on benches 20 feet away. All the activities took place in the windows, the door and on the roof of the building. In some of the windows were live performers, in others, film and in others, shadows of performers. Blueprint was a living frieze of activity and sound. The beginnings of my ideas about architecture as structure, simultaneous realities, cinematic scale, and performance as direct experience, could be glimpsed in the piece.

– Meredith Monk

Meredith
Monk

Don Preston silhouetted
in the window.

"I was trying to break down habitual ways of thinking about the act of going to performance. I made pieces to be performed at different times of day or pieces that took place over a period of time in different locations, incorporating memory as part of the experience."

— Meredith Monk

Juice:
a theatre cantata in three installments

1969, Sites: The Guggenheim Museum,
Minor Latham Playhouse,
and The House Loft, New York City.
For 85 performers.

Juice (1969), one of Monk's most important site-specific works, was performed at three different locations over a month and a half period. Audiences moved with the performers within and between each site. Monk's concept was a zoom lens: the viewer's perception of the piece shifted from the monumental to the intimate during the progression of the piece from site to site. Part I of *Juice* took place at the Solomon R. Guggenheim Museum in New York. Elements of the piece included a woman on horseback; 85 singer-dancers in red combat boots performing activities on the museum's spiraling ramps (where an exhibiton on Roy Lichtenstein was installed): and a group of four principal performers, their red-painted bodies intertwined, moving through the space as one figure. A month later, Part II was presented at Barnard College's Minor Latham Playhouse. Elements from the first part of the piece were revisited, in reduced and intensified form: a toy rocking horse was substituted for the real horse; a Lichtenstein poster hanging inside a log cabin stood in for the museum exhibition; and the four characters that had been connected in Part I became separate figures. Part III took place a week later at Monk's loft in lower Manhattan. Here, audience members walked into an installation of all the objects and costumes used in the previous two parts. The artifacts of the piece could be touched, smelled and experienced at close range while four characters that had been the focus of Parts I and II were now only visible on videotape as giant faces talking about performing the piece.

— Siri Engberg

Above, *Juice* 1st installment. Performers on the ramps of the Guggenheim Museum.

Above, *Juice* 2nd installment. Below, *Juice* 3rd installment.

Needlebrain Lloyd and The Systems Kid:
a live movie

1970, Sites: Various locations, Connecticut College,
New London, Connecticut.
For 150 performers.

*Needlebrain Lloyd and the Systems Kid
was first presented in 1970. Spread over
the course of an entire day and evening,
the performance included images
ranging from the rowing of a boat on
a lake to a Land Rover filled with
performers driving around the perimeter
of a huge green to horses galloping
across a field to motorcycles circling
the audience. Monk saw the piece as a
kind of "painting of events," playing with
scale and images as if they were in
the context of cinema.*

— Siri Engberg

*I have always been interested in film as
syntax and as a way of combining
images, music and movement within one
form. In 1970, I wanted to make a large
non-narrative film of dreamlike images in
constantly shifting landscapes but it was
obvious that I would not find the financial
means to do that. I began thinking about
how I could work with some of those
ideas in a live performance. I had been
investigating the performer/audience
relationship in terms of scale and
proximity. I decided to work with
cinematic concepts such as close-ups,
disjunctions of time and space, pans,
zooms, and dissolves as inspiration for
weaving together events in a piece to
take place in four different outdoor
spaces.*

— Meredith Monk

Vessel
an opera epic

1971, Sites: Meredith Monk's loft, The Performing Garage, and Wooster Street parking lot, New York City.
For 75 performers.

Vessel: an opera epic was originally performed in 1971. Characterized as "a performance tapestry," the three-part work was loosely based on the life of Joan of Arc. Each part was performed at a different New York location: Monk's loft, a garage theater, and a parking lot. Audience members were bussed from site to site. In 1980, Monk revived the piece for the Schaubühne Ensemble of West Berlin. There the audience traveled from a club in Kreuzberg to the Schaubühne Theater, and finally to the Anhalter Bahnhof, the remnant of a railroad station bombed in World War II. Images in the piece included pioneers at campfires, motorcycles, a Volkswagen bus inhabited by colorful revelers, two armies, a monster, a welder, a children's court, and a harvest dance performed by the entire cast.

– Siri Engberg

I thought of Vessel literally as an epic. We rented a bus to take the audience from my loft on Great Jones Street where they had seen Part I: Open House to the Performing Garage for Part II: Handmade Mountain. Parts I and II were performed on the weekday nights. We could only fit 100 people in my loft so on the weekend, we performed Part III: Existent Lot in an abandoned parking lot for all the people who had been to the other two parts during the week.

– Meredith Monk

Vessel Part I. Left, Berlin revival. Right, Lanny Harrison on the fire escape of Monk's loft.

Above, *Vessel Part II*. Berlin revival. Below, *Vessel Part III*, New York City.

American Archeology #1: Roosevelt Island

1994, Sites: Lighthouse Park, Renwick Ruin,
Roosevelt Island, New York City.
For 70 performers.

American Archeology #1 was created
by Monk in 1991 to be performed on
Roosevelt Island, a strip of land in New
York's East River that was once the site of
prisons, poorhouse, and hospitals. Two
sites on the island were used for the
performance, which emphasized the
intersection between past and present. In
the first section, performed in Lighthouse
Park, spectators sat on a slope and
observed various actions, from strolling
pedestrians wearing period costumes to
children at play to a galloping horse and
rider. The second section took place at
night at an abandoned smallpox
hospital. Images included: laboring
convicts, homeless people, doctors and
patients, and an archeologist. The piece
ended in a processional dominated by a
giant skeleton, followed by the
appearance of the horse and a Native
American rider on the crest of a hill.

– Siri Engberg

*In American Archeology #1, I was
inspired by a place that had always
been designated as a site for outcasts
and criminals, the outsiders of society.
The notion of quarantine seemed to
contain many contemporary resonances
particularly with the outbreak of the AIDS
epidemic. Over the years, I have been
exploring the many different ways layers
of culture accumulate in and inform a
particular place.*

– Meredith Monk

Procession from *American Archeology #1* in front of the former Renwick Smallpox Hospital, Manhattan skyline in the background.

Drawings by Meredith Monk for *American Archeology #1*.

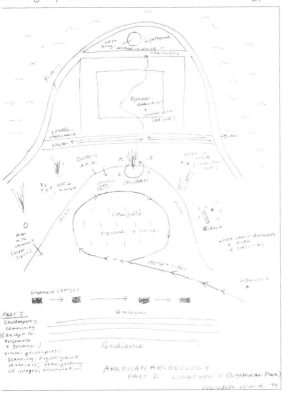

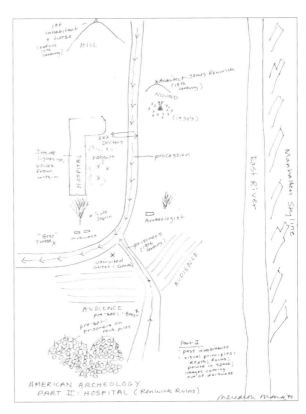

Rehearsal of *Vessel* Part III, Anhalter Bahnhof, Berlin, 1980.

I've always been interested in the mysterious and indefinable; seeing the familiar in a new way; crossing boundaries of how we normally perceive the world. I like to think that I am offering an experience that could be a template of expansiveness, of limitless possibility, of feeling more alive...

– Meredith Monk

All the site-specific works in this chapter were conceived, directed and composed by Meredith Monk.

Conclusion:
Documentation

> The reproduction of a painting or object, however perfect, is
> always, definitively, its betrayal. And that betrayal is that much
> greater when it involves not objects or paintings but whole spaces.
>
> (Buren 1991: 19)

In exploring site-specific art's unravelling of notions of original or fixed
location, this volume has addressed a range of practices in which the
more directly the site is pressed toward, the more elusive and complex
this point of definition proves to be. Here, in fact, site-specificity arises
precisely in uncertainties over the borders and limits of work and site.
In the writing of non-place over place, the troubling of oppositions
between virtual and real spaces, in the implication of the map in the
production of its object, the eroding of the material integrity of the art
object, and in the uncovering of processes of slippage, deferral and indeterminacy, these practices approach their various sites in a blurring of
the distinctions under which a work's integrity and place is fixed. Yet,
even as these various practices uncover a complex of events and
processes to which the site is subject, the questions, qualifications, and
implications of the specific site remain constantly in play. Indeed, the
documentations which are in exchange with this critical narrative testify
to this, as, in approaching this book as the site of performance's recovery
and recuperation, they work to expose its constraints.

It is for this reason that one of the first observations one might make
of each of these documentations is their sensitivity to their own limits,
their willingness to concede the impossibility of reproducing the object
toward which their statements, speculations, fragments, memories and
evocations are aimed. Yet, in this respect, these documents do not
simply reflect upon the apparent contradiction of attempting to record

site-specific works in another place, time, and through another medium, but act out some of the complexities of the relationship between work and site. It is in this context that Tim Etchells, for Forced Entertainment, narrates a process of approaching and passing through the sites for *Nights In This City*. Using an explicitly literary conceit to expose its ground, Etchells' documentation plays on the company's *moving on* from the city in *writing to* its sites. In *LE STANZE (THE ROOMS)*, Michelangelo Pistoletto presents documentation as an explicit instrument *in* and *of* the work, noting his anticipation, memory and loss of *LE STANZE*'s series of installations. Here, *LE STANZE* foregrounds the complex inter-dependence of its virtual and real spaces, in which 'each separate piece of writing is a functional part of the work itself', yet where these statements can be 'no more than a part of the engine and cannot be replaced by another gear'. For Brith Gof, Clifford McLucas elicits the viewer's participation in a documentation which emphasises the constraints of the documentary form and the structural complexity of the event it recalls. In foregrounding this tension, *Ten Feet and Three Quarters of an Inch of Theatre* takes on the properties of a notation, inviting the viewer to animate the material or 'to retain the charged erotics of incompletion by leaving things as they are – forever unfinished'. Julian Maynard Smith's address to Station House Opera's breeze block performances emphasises documentation's partial intervention into complex processes, foregrounding, for *The Bastille Dances*, snapshots of a vocabulary and process derived from the performers' physical exchange with specific materials. Subsequently, for *The Salisbury Proverbs*, Maynard Smith re-presents the disjunctive effect of a choreography created according to sculptural and architectural imperatives on metaphor and the unfolding of narrative. Finally, Meredith Monk presents a series of images reflecting her strongly compositional concerns and approach to site through formal difference and disjunction. Here, Monk's documentation reflects upon her address to the phenomenological *limitlessness* of 'real' space by explicitly tracing the structures and vocabularies of film and performance over sites they cannot contain. Consistently with the tactics and events of which they are an index, each of these documentations foregrounds its own limits, so admitting the recuperation of site-specific performance at *this site* into their subject matter and process.

Yet, even as they foreground the dislocation defining documentation's relationship to its object, these presentations recall approaches to sites subject to recollection and anticipation, process and event, evoking the 'absences' (Eisenman 1986: 6) at play in the event of site-specificity itself. Indeed, in these works, *the site* is not assumed to be simply *present to* performance or necessarily *absent from* documentation. This is a relationship reflected in works which explicitly incorporate processes of 'documentation' into approaches to site or even effect a site-specificity in exchanges between documentation and event. In asserting that the Non-Site operates as a 'limited mapped revision' (Smithson 1996a: 104) in 'the absence of the site' (Lippard and Smithson 1996: 193), Robert Smithson explicitly utilised and elaborated a documentation rephrased as *mapping*. Here, where the site cannot be read, represented, or thought without the very mapping which threatens its erasure, the site's *documentation* is used to foreground the paradoxes of representation itself. Earth art, land art, and subsequently body art, similarly came to treat the gallery as a place to document or map interventions into inaccessible sites, or, for Dennis Oppenheim, to perform a mapping of one site into another. Documentation also plays a role in otherwise formally diverse kinds of site-specific practice. The relationship between Krzysztof Wodiczko's large-scale projections and their photographic documentation mirrors that between the images he employs and their architectural hosts. In being 'recorded and announced' through the media as an 'urban event' (Wodiczko 1992: 196), Wodiczko's projections are absorbed back into the economy of images on which he draws. Yet, in remembering the 'missing' image, the 'missing' part, this media-documentation continues to 'write over' the city's spaces, becoming yet another 'repertoire of iconography' in which its meanings are produced. Deploying documentation in another way, Pistoletto shows a photographic documentation of *LE STANZE*'s first installation as the object of the second, concluding that 'overthrowing the medium [. . .] makes us more sensitive to the previous experience'. Monk's *Juice* traces out an analogous process, in which one performance space and event comes to stand in for another. Paradoxically, these strategies suggest, whether in the work or subsequent to it, documentation has a place within site-specific practice precisely because it explicitly presents itself in the absence of its object.

As this implies, where they work to foreground their limits, the tactics of a site-specific work and its documentation may find an affinity. Indeed, just as the documentations presented to this book tend to emphasise the displacements operating through their recollection of ephemeral events, so site-specific practice invariably works to expose that which confines it. To this end, in *LE STANZE*, Pistoletto approaches the 'real' rooms *in* the limits of documentation, reminding us that 'in "overturning" a medium to serve creative expression, it not only becomes useful, but also declares its limits, its fragility, its precariousness'. Such site-specific work incorporates documentation precisely in order to address the paradoxical relationship between its construction of a work and the site it seeks to uncover. Here, in fact, just as Tschumi addresses the reading of architecture in order to reveal that architecture cannot be reduced to a text, so Pistoletto deploys documentation in and through *LE STANZE* in order to expose and utilise its *restless* relationship with the event it recalls.

Yet this correspondence can go even further. Just as site-specificity arises in a blurring of the opposition between a work and its contexts, so, where documentation is a tactic of the site-specific work, the distinctions between *documentation* and *notation*, between that which is *remembered* and *anticipated*, *recorded* and *produced* may come under question.

In Tschumi's architectural practice, this upsetting of oppositions is reflected in the relationship between architectural theory and practice. Indeed, in approaching Tschumi's design for La Villette, it is in this context that one might read the functioning of the built *Folies*. Positioned according to the 'system of points', one of the three autonomous systems defining the structure of the park, the distribution and

permutation of these 'points of intensity' offer an allusion to the functioning of a text. Distributed according to an arbitrary grid across the
whole area of the park, and constructed through the repetition and variation of a basic built structure, the *Folies* present a series of deviations
from an implied architectural norm. In this 'system' created through
relations of 'difference', the *Folie* alludes to the functioning of the signifier. Indeed, as the *Folies* are subject to the other conflicting systems
defining the park's uses, so they are designed to 'receive the play of
signs' (Tschumi 1985: 3) and to be defined according to different uses
at different times. Here, Tschumi concludes, as a 'construction of
neutral space', the *Folie* becomes an 'empty house', the '*case vide*',

> an empty slot or box in a chart or matrix, an unoccupied square
> in a chessboard, a blank compartment: the point of the
> unexpected, before data entered on the vertical axis can meet
> with data on the horizontal one.
>
> (Tschumi 1985: 3)

In this context, the architect and critic Anthony Vidler suggests,
Tschumi effects a deconstruction of the opposition between architectural theory and practice, as, in reproducing the functioning of the
signifier, the *Folies* offer a 'built notation', rather than a resolution
of an architectural notation *in* a built form. Whereas in traditional
practice, he argues,

> the notations of the plan, elevation, section, geometrical and
> perspectival projection, are accepted *as* notations; they refer to
> something else, concrete and tangible in the realm of the
> building. In Tschumi [. . .] what were in one frame of reference,
> recognizable as merely notations, become indeed, built notations.
> The result is that the work on notation is quite literally,
> constructed.
>
> (Vidler 1988: 21)

It is here that La Villette sets the conditions for its specificity to site, where the *Folies* provide points of intensity and temporary resolution for a performance of architecture and site in its multiple and diverse *uses*.

Where the *Folie*, as 'notation', empties itself in anticipation of its use, documentation works to efface itself in favour of that which it recalls. In this sense, both notation and documentation act out a displacement intrinsic to this site-specific practice. In approaching the site as a set of terms always *in play*, the site-specific work inevitably operates *in anticipation* or *in recollection* of the places it acts out. Indeed, it is in this context that Tschumi asserts La Villette's 'anticontextual' nature (Tschumi 1987: VII) as he seeks to define an architecture and site whose meaning is always subject to performance, always yet to be defined. Here, too, documentation, in declaring itself to be always other to the events and objects it recalls, finds a direct affinity with the tactics and processes underpinning site-specific practice. Finally, it is to this end that site-specific art so persistently works against its own final or definitive location, as, through this wide variety of forms and strategies, it speculates toward the performance of its places.

Bibliography

Acconci, V. (1972) 'Notes on Work' *Avalanche* 6: 1–78.
—— (1975 [1970]) 'Adaptation Studies' in Richard Kostalanetz (ed.) *Essaying Essays: Alternative Forms of Exposition*, New York: Out of London Press, 190–5.
—— (1978) *Vito Acconci*, Luzern: Kunstmuseum Luzern.
—— (1982) *Recorded documentation by Vito Acconci of the exhibition and commissioning for San Diego State University*, San Diego, Cal.: San Diego State University (audio cassette).
—— (1993) *The City Inside Us*, Vienna: Peter Noever, MAK.
—— (1996 [1970]) 'Rubbing Piece' in Nick Kaye (ed.) *Art into Theatre: Performance Interviews and Documents*, Amsterdam: Harwood Academic Press, 65.
Alloway, L. (1981) 'Sites/Non-Sites' in Robert Hobbs (ed.) *Robert Smithson: Sculpture*, London: Cornell University Press, 41–6.
Amann, J.-C. (ed.) (1976) *Gilberto Zorio*, Luzern: Kunstmuseum Luzern (pages unnumbered).
—— (1977) *Giuseppe Penone*, Luzern: Kunstmuseum Luzern.
Anselmo, G. (1989) *Giovanni Anselmo*, Florence: Hopeful Monster.
—— (1996) interview with Nick Kaye translated by Gabriella Giannachi, Turin, 17 December.
Augé, M. (1995) *Non-Places: Introduction to an Anthropology of Supermodernity*, London: Verso.
Banes, S. (1978) 'The Art of Meredith Monk', *Performing Arts Journal* 3, 1: 3–18.
Bear, L. and Monk, M. (1997 [1976]) 'Meredith Monk: Invocation/Evocation' in Deborah Jowitt (ed.) *Meredith Monk*, Baltimore: Johns Hopkins University Press, 79–93.
Bear, L. and Sharp, W. (1996 [1970]) 'Discussions with Heizer, Oppenheim, Smithson' in Jack Flam (ed.) *Robert Smithson: The Collected Writings*, Berkeley, Cal.: University of California Press, 242–52.
Becker, H.S. and Walton, J. (1975) 'Social Science and the Work of Hans Haacke' in Hans Haacke *Framing and Being Framed: 7 Works*, Halifax, Nova Scotia: Nova Scotia College of Art and Design, 145–52.
Benjamin, A. (1988) 'Derrida, Architecture and Philosophy', *Architectural Design* 58, 3–4: 8–11.
Bernhardt, E. *et al.* (1994) *On Site Specific Performance*, New York: New York Public Library for the Performing Arts (video recording).

Buren, D. (1973) *Five Texts*, London: John Weber Gallery and John Wendle Gallery.

—— (1976) *THE CUBE THE WHITE THE IDEALISM (1967–1975) followed by 'GOING THROUGH' a guide for the two exhibitions 'TO TRANSGRESS' and 'TO PLACE' respectively and simultaneously visible at THE LEO CASTELLI GALLERY and THE JOHN WEBER GALLERY 420 West Broadway, New York, September 1976*, New York: Leo Castelli Gallery and John Weber Gallery (pages unnumbered).

—— (1991) *The Square of The Flags*, Helsinki: Helsinki Museum of Contemporary Art.

Burnham, J. (1975) 'Steps in the Formulation of Real-Time Political Art' in Hans Haacke *Framing and Being Framed: 7 Works*, Halifax, Nova Scotia: Nova Scotia College of Art and Design, 127–44.

Cage, J. (1968) *Silence: Lectures and Writings*, London: Marion Boyars.

Cage, J. and Charles, D. (1981) *For the Birds*, London: Marion Boyars.

Castagnotto, U. (1976) 'Electricity as Expressive Tension' in Jean-Christofe Amann (ed.) *Gilberto Zorio*, Luzern: Kunstmuseum Luzern (pages unnumbered).

Celant, G. (1967) 'Arte povera: appunti per una guerriglia', *Flash Art 5*.

—— (ed.) (1969) *Art Povera: Conceptual, Actual or Impossible Art?*, London: Studio Vista.

—— (1989) *Penone*, Milan: Electa.

—— (1991) *Gilberto Zorio*, Florence: Hopeful Monster.

Christov-Bakargiev, C. (1987) 'Arte Povera 1967–1987', *Flash Art* (international edition) 137: 52–69.

Compton, M. and Sylvester, D. (1971) *Robert Morris*, London: Tate Gallery.

Cora, B. (1995) 'Michelangelo Pistoletto: From the Mirror Paintings to Progetto Arte. The Artist as Sponsor of Thought' in Michelangelo Pistoletto *Pistoletto: Le Porte di Palazzo Fabroni*, Milan: Charta, 41–55.

Crimp, D. (1993) *On the Museum's Ruins*, London: MIT Press.

de Certeau, M. (1984) *The Practice of Everyday Life*, Berkeley, Cal.: University of California Press.

Debord, G. (1981 [1956]) 'Theory of the Derive' in Ken Knabb (ed.) *Situationist International Anthology*, Berkeley, Cal.: Bureau of Public Secrets, 50–54.

Derrida, J. (1974) *Of Grammatology*, London: Johns Hopkins University Press.

—— (1985) 'Point de Folie – Maintenant L'Architecture' in Bernard Tschumi *La Case Vide*, London: Architectural Association, 4–19.

Deutsche, R. (1996) *Evictions: Art and Spatial Politics*, Cambridge, Mass.: MIT Press.

Eisenman, P. (1986) *Moving Arrows, Eros and Other Errors: An Architecture of Absence*, London: Architectural Association.

Etchells, T. (1994) 'Diverse assembly: some trends in recent performance' in
  Theodore Shank (ed.) *Contemporary British Theatre*, London: Macmillan
  Press, 107–22.

—— (1995) *Nights in this City* (unpublished manuscript).

—— (1999 [1995]) 'Eight Fragments on Theatre and the City' in Tim Etchells
  Certain Fragments: Contemporary Performance and Forced Entertainment,
  London: Routledge, 76–81.

Flam, J. (ed.) (1996) *Robert Smithson: The Collected Writings*, Berkeley, Cal.:
  University of California Press.

Fried, M. (1968) 'Art and Objecthood' in Gregory Battcock (ed.) *Minimal Art:
  A Critical Anthology*, New York: E.P. Dutton, 116–47.

Goossen, E.C. (1973 [1958]) 'The Big Canvas' in Gregory Battcock (ed.) *The
  New Art*, New York: E.P. Dutton, 57–65.

Greenberg, C. (1962) 'After Abstract Expressionism', *Art International* 6, 8:
  26–30.

Haacke, H. (1975) *Framing and Being Framed: 7 Works*, Halifax, Nova Scotia:
  Nova Scotia College of Art and Design.

Hansen, A. (1965) *A Primer of Happenings and Space-Time Art*, New York:
  Something Else Press.

Hapgood, B. (1994) *Neo-Dada: Redefining Art 1958–62*, New York: American
  Federation of Arts and Universal Publishing.

Heiss, A. (1992) *Dennis Oppenheim: Selected Works 1967–1990*, New York: Harry
  N. Abrams Inc.

Higgins, D. (1969 [1966]) 'Intermedia' in Dick Higgins *foew&ombwhhw*, New
  York: Something Else Press, 11–29.

Hobbs, R. (ed.) (1981) *Robert Smithson: Sculpture*, London: Cornell University
  Press.

Jameson, F. (1986) 'Hans Haacke and the Cultural Logic of Postmodernism' in
  Brian Wallis (ed.) *Hans Haacke: Unfinished Business*, Cambridge, Mass.:
  MIT Press, 39–50.

Jameson, F. (1991) *Postmodernism, or, The Cultural Logic of Late Capitalism*,
  London: Verso.

Jencks, C. (1987) *Post-Modernism: The New Classicism in Art and Architecture*,
  London: Academy Editions.

Jowitt, D. (ed.) (1997) *Meredith Monk*, London: Johns Hopkins University
  Press.

Kaprow, A. (1966) *Assemblages, Environments, and Happenings*, New York: Harry
  N. Abrams Inc.

—— (1966a) *Some Recent Happenings*, New York: Something Else Press.

—— (1993 [1958]) 'The Legacy of Jackson Pollock' in Allan Kaprow *Essays on
  the Blurring of Art and Life* edited by Jeff Kelley, Berkeley, Cal.: University
  of California Press, 1–9.

—— (1993a [1958]) 'Notes on the Creation of a Total Art' in Allan Kaprow *Essays on the Blurring of Art and Life* edited by Jeff Kelley, Berkeley, Cal.: University of California Press, 10–12.

—— (1993b [1963]) 'Impurity' in Allan Kaprow *Essays on the Blurring of Art and Life* edited by Jeff Kelley, Berkeley, Cal.: University of California Press, 27–45.

—— (1993c [1971]) 'The Education of the Un-Artist, Part 1' in Allan Kaprow *Essays on the Blurring of Art and Life* edited by Jeff Kelley, Berkeley, Cal.: University of California Press, 97–109.

—— (1995 [1965]) 'Calling' in Mariellen R. Sandford (ed.) *Happenings and Other Acts*, London: Routledge, 195–201.

Kaprow, A. and Schechner, R. (1968) 'Extensions in Time and Space', *Drama Review* 12, 2: 153–9.

Kaye, N. (1994) *Postmodernism and Performance*, London: Macmillan Press.

—— (ed.) (1996) *Art into Theatre: Performance Interviews and Documents*, Amsterdam: Harwood Academic Press.

Klotz, H. (1988) *The History of Postmodern Architecture*, Cambridge, Mass.: MIT Press.

Koenig, C. (1976) 'Meredith Monk: Performer-Creator', *Drama Review* 20, 3: 51–66.

Kostalanetz, R. (ed.) (1980 [1968]) *The Theatre of Mixed Means*, New York: RK Editions.

Kwon, M. (1997) 'One Place After Another: Notes on Site Specificity', *October* 80: 85–110.

Lajer-Burcharth, E. (1987) 'Urban Disturbances', *Art in America* 75, 11:146–53, 197.

Lefebvre, H. (1991) *The Production of Space*, Oxford: Blackwells.

Linker, K. (1994) *Vito Acconci*, New York: Rizzoli.

Lippard, L.R. and Smithson, R. (1996 [1973]) 'Fragments of an Interview with P.A. [Patsy] Norvell' in Jack Flam (ed.) *Robert Smithson: The Collected Writings*, Berkeley, Cal.: University of California Press, 192–5.

Lippert, W. (1976) 'About Gilberto Zorio' in Jean-Christofe Amann (ed.) *Gilberto Zorio*, Luzern: Kunstmuseum Luzern (pages unnumbered).

Lynch, K. (1960) *The Image of the City*, Cambridge, Mass.: MIT Press.

Martin, L. (1990) 'Transpositions: On the Intellectual Origins of Tschumi's Architectural Theory', *Assemblage* 11: 23–36.

Maynard Smith, J. (1996) 'Drunken Madness' in Nick Kaye (ed.) *Art into Theatre: Performance Interviews and Documents*, Amsterdam: Harwood Academic Press, 198–200.

McEvilley, T. (1992) 'The Rightness of Wrongness: Modernism and Its Alter-Ego in the Work of Dennis Oppenheim' in Alanna Heiss *Dennis Oppenheim: Selected Works 1967–1990*, New York: Harry N. Abrams Inc., 7–76.

McLucas, C. (1996) letter to Nick Kaye, 3 June.

McLucas, C., Morgan, R. and Pearson, M. (1995) *Y Llyfyr Glas*, Cardiff: Brith Gof.

Monk, M. (1969) 'Notes for Juice' (programme notes).

Morris, R. (1993 [1966]) 'Notes on Sculpture, Part 1' in Robert Morris *Continuous Project Altered Daily: The Writings of Robert Morris*, London: MIT Press, 1–10.

—— (1993a [1966]) 'Notes on Sculpture, Part 2' in Robert Morris *Continuous Project Altered Daily: The Writings of Robert Morris*, London: MIT Press, 11–22.

—— (1993b [1968]) 'Anti-Form' in Robert Morris *Continuous Project Altered Daily: The Writings of Robert Morris*, London: MIT Press, 41–51.

—— (1993c [1978]) 'The Present Tense of Space' in Robert Morris *Continuous Project Altered Daily: The Writings of Robert Morris*, London: MIT Press, 175–210.

—— (1993d) 'Notes on Sculpture, Part 4: Beyond Objects' in Robert Morris *Continuous Project Altered Daily: The Writings of Robert Morris*, London: MIT Press, 51–70.

—— (1997) interview with Nick Kaye, New York, 8 April.

Nesmer, C. (1971) ' An Interview with Vito Acconci', *Arts Magazine* 45, 5: 20–23.

O'Docherty, B. (1986 [1976]) *Inside the White Cube: The Ideology of the Gallery Space*, San Francisco: Lapis Press.

Oldenburg, C. (1965) 'A Statement' in Michael Kirby (ed.) *Happenings: An Anthology*, New York: E.P. Dutton Inc., 200–3.

—— (1967) *Store Days*, New York: Something Else Press.

—— (1973) *Raw Notes*, Halifax, Nova Scotia: Nova Scotia College of Art and Design.

Oldenburg, C., Lichtenstein, R. and Warhol, A. (1966) 'Oldenburg, Lichtenstein, Warhol: A Discussion', *Artforum* 4, 6: 20–4.

Onions, C.T. (ed.) *The Shorter Oxford English Dictionary*, Oxford: Clarendon Press.

Oppenheim, D. (1969) *Gallery Decomposition*, New York: John Weber Gallery (gallery announcement).

Penone, G. (1996) interview with Nick Kaye translated by Gabriella Giannachi, Turin, 18 December.

Plant, S. (1992) *The Most Radical Gesture: The Situationist International in a Postmodern Age*, London: Routledge.

Ponti, L.L. (1990) 'La Biennale di Venezia 1990', *Domus*, 718: 66–79.

Rainer, Y. (1974 [1968]) 'A Quasi Survey of Some "Minimalist" Tendencies in the Quantitatively Minimal Dance Activity Midst the Plethora, or an Analysis of *Trio A*' in Yvonne Rainer *Work 1961–73*, Halifax, Nova Scotia: Nova Scotia College of Art and Design, 63–74.

Rogers, S. (1988) 'Showing the Wires: Interview with Julian Maynard Smith', *Performance Magazine* 56–7: 9–14.

Rosenberg, H. (1959) *The Tradition of the New*, New York: Horizon Press.

Sanouillet, M. and Peterson, E. (eds) (1975) *The Essential Writings of Marcel Duchamp*, London: Thames & Hudson.

Serra, R. (1994 [1969]) '*Tilted Arc* Destroyed' in Richard Serra *Writings Interviews*, Chicago: Chicago University Press, 193–214.

Shapiro, G. (1995) *Earthwards: Robert Smithson and Art After Babel*, Berkeley, Cal.: University of California Press.

Sharp, W. (1970) 'Body Works: A pre-critical, non-definitive survey of very recent works using the human body or parts thereof', *Avalanche* 1: 1–4.

—— (1971) 'Dennis Oppenheim Interviewed by Willoughby Sharp', *Studio International* 183, 938: 186–93.

Smithson, R. (1996 [1967]) 'Towards the Development of an Air Terminal' in Jack Flam (ed.) *Robert Smithson: The Collected Writings*, Berkeley, Cal.: University of California Press, 52–60.

—— (1996a [1968]) 'A Sedimentation of the Mind: Earth Projects' in Jack Flam (ed.) *Robert Smithson: The Collected Writings*, Berkeley, Cal.: University of California Press, 100–13.

—— (1996b [1972]) 'The Spiral Jetty' in Jack Flam (ed.) *Robert Smithson: The Collected Writings*, Berkeley, Cal.: University of California Press, 143–53.

Smithson, R. and Toner, P. (1996) 'Interview with Robert Smithson' in Jack Flam (ed.) *Robert Smithson: The Collected Writings*, Berkeley, Cal.: University of California Press, 234–41.

Smithson, R. and Wheeler, D. (1996) 'Four Conversations Between Dennis Wheeler and Robert Smithson' in Jack Flam (ed.) *Robert Smithson: The Collected Writings*, Berkeley, Cal.: University of California Press, 196–233.

Sohm, H. (1970) *Happenings and Fluxus*, Cologne: Kölnischer Kunstverein (pages unnumbered).

Soja, E. W. (1989) *Postmodern Geographies: The Reassertion of Space in Critical Social Theory*, London: Verso.

Strickland, E. (1997 [1988]) 'Voices/Visions: An Interview with Meredith Monk' in Deborah Jowitt (ed.) *Meredith Monk*, Baltimore: Johns Hopkins University Press, 133–55.

Templeton, F. (1990) *YOU – The City*, New York: Roof Books.

Tschumi, B. (1985) *La Case Vide*, London: Architectural Association.

—— (1987) *Cinegram Folie Le Parc De La Villette*, Princeton: Princeton Architectural Press.

—— (1988) 'Parc de la Villette, Paris', *Architectural Design* 58, 3–4: 32–9.

—— (1994) *Architecture and Disjunction*, London: MIT Press.

—— (1994a [1975]) 'The Architectural Paradox' in Bernard Tschumi *Architecture and Disjunction*, London: MIT Press, 27–52.

—— (1994b [1976]) 'Architecture and Transgression' in Bernard Tschumi *Architecture and Disjunction*, London: MIT Press, 65–78.

—— (1994c [1980]) 'Architecture and Limits' in Bernard Tschumi *Architecture and Disjunction*, London: MIT Press, 101–18.

—— (1994d [1987]) 'Disjunctions' in Bernard Tschumi *Architecture and Disjunction*, London: MIT Press, 207–14.

Vidler, A. (1988) 'The Pleasure of the Architect', *Architecture and Urbanism* 216: 17–23.

Vostell, W. (1966) *dé-coll/age happenings* translated by Laura P. Williams, New York: Something Else Press.

—— (1968) *Miss Vietnam and texts of other happenings*, San Francisco: Nova Broadcast Press.

White, R. (ed.) (1979) 'Daniel Buren', *View* 1, 9: whole issue.

Wodiczko, K. (1986) 'Krzysztof Wodiczko', *Audio Arts Magazine*, side 1 (audio cassette).

—— (1992) *Krzysztof Wodiczko: Instruments, Projeccions, Vehicles*, Barcelona: Fundacio Antoni Tapies.

—— (1996) 'Projections' in Saskia Bos (ed.) *Krzysztof Wodiczko: De Appel Amsterdam 1996*, Amsterdam: De Appel Foundation, 54–7.

Wodiczko, K. and Ferguson, B.W. (1992) 'A Conversation with Krzysztof Wodiczko' in Krzysztof Wodiczko *Krzysztof Wodiczko: Instruments, Projeccions, Vehicles*, Barcelona: Fundacio Antoni Tapies, 47–66.

Zacharopolous, D. (1996) 'Gilberto Zorio' in Gilberto Zorio *Gilberto Zorio*, Turin: Hopeful Monster, 189–98.

Zorio, G. (1996) Interview with Nick Kaye, translated by Gabriella Giannachi, Turin, 20 December.

Index